ECCENTRICITY: SOCIETY'S SECRET SAUCE

The Value of Being Eccentric

By Brett Sinclair

Copyright 2016 Brett Sinclair

Alpha Academic Press

Published in the United States of America

COPYRIGHT DISCLAIMER

Eccentricity: Society's Secret Sauce
First Edition, Paperback
Published Date: March 2017
Alpha Academic Press
ISBN: 978-0-9975603-5-0

TABLE OF CONTENTS

Chapter 1

ECCENTRICITY: SOCIETY'S SECRET SAUCE

"The amount of eccentricity in a society has generally been proportional to the amount of genius, mental vigor, and moral courage which it contained,"

John Stuart Mill

INTRODUCTION

This is an unconventional book. It is partly a book on psychology and sociology because it delves into psychological and sociological perspectives. It is in part a history book but is not a traditional work of history even though the lives of historical figures are an integral part of *'Eccentricity: Society's Secret Sauce'*. So the book you are about to read is odd indeed because it focuses on *an infrequently examined and distinct category of people found within any society.*

Eccentrics are this distinct category of people found within any society. Eccentric people are commonly believed to constitute a very small minority of the many subsets of people that as a whole make up any given society. In addition to being regarded as a statistically insignificant category of people within any society, eccentric people are - solely because of their eccentricity - frequently disregarded, disparaged, and deemed incapable of making worthwhile contributions to the world they live in.

The idea that eccentrics have been vital forces behind the positive and beneficial advancement of society may seem ludicrous to some. Yet, eccentric people have throughout history often been the *'secret sauce'* responsible for leading the way with innovative advancements and positive contributions that enriched the world. Some are famous, some are not, but eccentric people have had a notable and often profound effect on society and on the lives of the people that their lives touched.

The title of this book is, '*Eccentricity: Society's Secret* Sauce'; but what is a *'society'*?

Before answering this question, it is important to note that whenever two or more words are joined to make a phrase, as in *'Society's Secret Sauce'*, the meaning of each word individually can be transformed or altered. An example of this happened to me on the first day of a trip to India in 1996, in the capital city of India, New Delhi. I was leaving Delhi the next morning for Calcutta (since 2001 known as Kolkata) for a month long sojourn there doing volunteer work in that impoverished city. But a taxi ride my wife and I took in New Delhi the evening before we flew to Calcutta seemed to ensure that neither of us would ever make it to Calcutta.

Our taxi driver was extremely talkative. After asking us where we wanted to go he talked incessantly. We just listened and sometimes were even able to get in a word edgewise. After telling us he was named 'taxi driver of the year' in Delhi, my wife asked me why he called the city Delhi instead of New Delhi and I explained to her that there were two parts to Delhi, the extremely poor 'Old Delhi' and 'New Delhi', a thriving and a relatively prosperous city. Then the taxi driver, perhaps because he felt ignored, began shouting at us: *"I am not a sick man! People keep saying, they tell me all the time that I am sick man, but I am not! I am not a sick man!"* We were both shocked by his vociferous statements and my wife thought we were about to die in a car crash!

My wife and I were however, both very concerned for our safety, so we talked about quickly getting out of the taxi the next time it was stopped for a red light. Then the taxi driver shouted loudly at us: *"It's because of my beard; my beard is why everyone tells me I am a sick man!"* Our taxi driver was obviously becoming even more agitated, so I moved a little closer to him and trying to calm him down, respectfully asked him why anyone would tell him he was a 'sick man' just because he had a beard. His mood changed almost instantly as he laughed and explained that he didn't mean that he was mentally sick or insane because he was not saying *'sick man'* but *'Sikh man'*, and then spelled out loud the word *'Sikh'*.

I had previously been to Amritsar, a city populated predominately by followers of the Sikh religion that is located in the Punjab region in northern India. I went to Amritsar to experience a distinct sub-culture within Indian society that was very different than the majority Hindu population in the rest of India, and, to see the famous *Golden Temple*. So, I was well aware of the fact that the *Sikhs* were Indians who as part of their religion never shaved their beards.

The misunderstanding in the taxi occurred because two words that we thought were *'sick'* and *'man'* were joined into a phrase that is often used to mean that someone is psychologically or mentally disturbed. But it is also commonly used to mean that a person is very ill physically, and by itself the word *'sick'* could be used in many different ways, for example, *'I'm sick of my job'*. Therefore, the context in which any word or phrase is used is often the only way to know which meaning of a word or a phrase is the intended meaning.

Leaving India and returning now to the meaning of the phrase *'Society's Secret Sauce'*, let's first examine the word *'society'*. When the word *'society'* is used it can be used in multiple contexts. For example, the phrase *'high society'*, is frequently deemed to be a certain class of people who are usually celebrities, rich, or famous. The word *'society'* as used in this book is meant to reflect the following primary definition from the Oxford English Dictionary:

society   1. The aggregate of people living together in a more or less ordered community; a particular community of people.

Having now defined the intended meaning of the word 'society' as used in the title of this book, *'Eccentricity: Society's Secret Sauce'*, let's examine the phrase *'secret* sauce'. When this phrase is used it's most common usage involves food. For example, when people dine with friends in a restaurant and find the chili they are eating exceptionally tasty, it is not uncommon for them to ask the chef what special ingredient was used in their chili that made it especially appealing to the palate. If the chef is available to speak with these inquisitive patrons of the restaurant, he or she will usually thank them for the compliment and oftentimes reply that it is a 'special ingredient' kept secret, a *'secret sauce'*.

The concept of a *'secret sauce'* is of course not confined to a restaurant with only one location. In fact, international restaurant chains have built their marketing concept around the advertising strategy of a *'secret sauce'* that differentiates their product and makes it taste better than their competitors' food.

KFC, originally called *Kentucky Fried Chicken*, claimed that their chicken was a secret mixture of eleven different herbs and spices and that this is the reason why their fried chicken tastes like no other fried chicken. *KFC* keeps the content of these eleven different herbs and spices a closely guarded corporate secret, but they have built their advertising campaign around the concept of their 'secret ingredients'. This marketing strategy has been so successful that *Kentucky Fried Chicken* started out with one location in Louisville, Kentucky, and even before changing their name to *KFC*, through the use of their *'secret sauce'* marketing strategy, prospered and expanded until they became the phenomenally successful KFC international restaurant chain with locations worldwide. *But what on earth does this brief history of KFC fried chicken have to do with eccentricity? The answer will quickly be forthcoming, but first:*

Beans anyone? About the most exciting things you can say about beans is that there are always plenty of them. But, In the United States, *Bush's Baked Beans* advertises extensively that the reason their canned baked beans are exceptionally tasty is due to the *'secret sauce'* present in each can of beans. Like *KFC, Bush's Baked Beans* has made their *'secret ingredient'* marketing strategy the cornerstone of their very successful national advertising campaign. You might at this point want to direct choice expletives to the author for this foray into *KFC* chicken and *Bush's Baked Beans. So what does KFC and Bush's Baked Beans use of the phrase 'secret sauce' in their marketing campaigns have to do with eccentricity?* The answer is that both *KFC* and *Bush's Baked Beans* understand and have capitalized on the following centuries old truth, followed by its relevant concomitant corollary:

Throughout history that which is <u>unique</u> has been greatly valued.

Eccentric people are unique.

Hoping that you are not now so hungry that you need to grab some delectably delicious delicacies to eat as you read on, let's return to the main subject of this book. Society also has its own 'secret sauce', a 'special ingredient' that countless times has been the reason behind the advancement and progress of society in a very beneficial way. These positive and diverse contributions to society have often been made through the conduit of a uniquely distinct factor, the metaphorical *'secret sauce'* of *eccentricity.*

People have often asked variations of the following question: *Why did, for example, Albert Einstein, John Lennon and Winston Churchill rise to the pinnacle of the respective fields they worked in while other equally talented people have not?*

There are multiple answers to this question. Common sense quickly generates a couple of logical and obvious answers. One of course is the reality that through no fault of our own, no matter how hard we tried or the depth of passion that we poured into our efforts, luck, timing, and circumstances beyond our control thwarted the success of our venture. As an aside, we should never be dismayed by failure, because failure is a steppingstone on the road to eventual success if we never give up. Colonel Sanders, the man who started *KFC*, was for most of his life an abject failure at every business he tried. It wasn't until he was 65 years old that he created the unique taste of *KFC* chicken and opened his first *Kentucky Fried Chicken* restaurant.

The second answer to our question: *Why did, for example, Albert Einstein, John Lennon and Winston Churchill rise to the pinnacle of the respective fields they worked in while others have not?, is* also logical and a matter of common sense that usually springs to mind with alacrity and is the focus of this book: *There must be something special and unique about people like Albert Einstein, John Lennon and Winston Churchill that fueled their success.*

There was indeed something special and unique that *Albert Einstein, Winston Churchill* and *John Lennon* all had in common. *They were all* **eccentric people**.

The plethora of eccentric people in the world is much larger than it is commonly thought to be. If the number of eccentrics in the world were in the thousands or even hundreds of thousands, a credible argument could be made that eccentric people couldn't possibly constitute a ubiquitous *'secret sauce'* endemic to society. While no mathematical accounting of the number of eccentric people in the world exists, largely due to the few times the subject of eccentricity has been studied and written about, the analysis of the attributes of eccentric people that is at the heart of this book suggests that the actual number of eccentric people in the world might be in the millions or even billions.

Society's Secret Sauce: Eccentric People.

When this word, 'eccentric', familiar to most people, comes to mind, what does it mean? What does it mean to you personally? If asked to define the word without the use of a dictionary, very common and typical responses would be: 'A person who is odd or unusual or quirky, someone possibly insane, possibly merely an individual with habits or a manner of behaving that is quite different than other people'. And, more often than not, if asked whether being eccentric is a desirable quality or not, the answer would be undesirable, and not a quality that most people would aspire to possessing.

But if asked to name positive traits in people, fairly common answers would be to mention things like loving one's family, being successful in life, being a kind and loving person, or someone who cares not only about himself or herself but their community and country, or someone who brings happiness to the lives of others, or, on a larger scale, plays a part in the advancement of peace in the world or in alleviating the suffering that is an unfortunate aspect of the world we live in. But being 'eccentric' is not usually thought of in a similarly positive way. In fact, being eccentric is generally not a quality most people would seek to make a part of what defines them as an individual.

Although there are a paucity of books published on the subject of eccentricity, what you are about to read challenges commonly held beliefs about eccentric people. One of those beliefs is that eccentrics are *not* considered to be people who have made great contributions to the world in fields as diverse as government, art, or science to name but a few. So what does it really mean to be *'eccentric'?*

Are eccentric people little more than weird people who usually find their place among the dregs of society? For example, what would you think about a man with a good job and income, who could easily afford to buy his own pack of cigarettes (in an era before the health risks of smoking were known), who picked up filthy, half smoked cigarette butts off the streets and sidewalks and lit them and smoked them? Probably not too much, until you discovered that one man history records who did this very thing routinely was the brilliant physicist Albert Einstein! This fact was reported by The Daily Telegraph on November 6th, 2005, and by UPI in Brussels, Belgium. Bernhard Caesar Einstein said in 1998 that in a letter written to him by Albert Einstein, his grandfather told him that he collected the cigarette butts to circumvent his doctor's orders to stop smoking.

While studying the very few psychological and sociological studies that have previously examined the subject of eccentricity, close to twenty personality attributes of eccentric people have been postulated by prior research, but of these there are only seven distinct personality attributes of eccentric people that are credible. These seven attributes and the reason for their number being seven will soon be carefully examined in this book, but for now they are merely listed below to acquaint you with them:

(1) Nonconforming attitude

(2) Creative

(3) Intense curiosity

(4) Idealistic

(5) Highly intelligent

(6) Opinionated

(7) Outspoken

There have been a few psychological and sociological theories that have been proposed since the early 19th century about eccentric people. However, *consider the fact that psychological and sociological theories of eccentric people are simply that: theories which may or may not be true. Statistics can be manipulated to 'prove' even the most absurd theories!*

Perhaps you have encountered personally, or as a college or graduate school student, or by reading a book, scholars well regarded in their fields who used statistics to prove absurd ideas. One incident I experienced was in a Communications Masters program in a class called *'Gender & Communication'*. The PhD professor 'proved' that there are no differences due to gender in the way that married couples communicated with each other. This study was done before same sex marriage was legalized in the United States so confined itself to heterosexual marriages. The professor 'proved' that married couples communicate with each other in the same way, and by using the same communication techniques, and that there is no difference in how they communicated with each other due to the fact that one spouse was male and the other spouse female.

Challenging this professor's *'statistically significant'* proof, I asked this professor what the professor's research was based upon. This inquiry was met with the reply that hundreds of people comprised the pool of people that led to the professor's 'discovery'. I wasn't satisfied with such a generic explanatory reply, so I asked the professor to be more specific with respect to these hundreds of people that provided the professor with the raw data that was then extrapolated upon through the principles of statistics to reach a 'scientific' conclusion. I was told in an authoritative and almost contemptuous manner that the raw data pool was based upon a few hundred questionnaires given to freshman and sophomore college students.

Upon further questioning of the professor by me, while I was respectful it was also clearly understood by this professor that my continued questioning was adversarial in nature, just as it should be, because the Socratic method of exchanging opposing ideas always is a much better method of learning than being a sycophant that blindly accepts whatever a college professor tells their class. Being a persistent fellow, I was finally able to have the professor reticently reveal to me and the entire class that not only was the raw data obtained from freshman and sophomore college students, over 90% of these students filled out the questionnaire because they were either required to, or did so to better their grade in a different class in the Communication department that they were taking that semester. Not only that, under 1% of these students that filled out this questionnaire were married!

Therefore, the probative value of the professor's raw data pool and conclusions reached from that raw data were about as accurate as information gathered about living conditions in Zimbabwe from a pool of Americans who have never once traveled outside of the United States. Having made several trips to Zimbabwe doing volunteer work there, this nation in southern Africa that was colonized by the British and used to be called Rhodesia has now been ruled for over 30 years by the dictator Robert Mugabe, and extreme poverty, hunger and death are the pervasive norm in Zimbabwe. Only the people of Zimbabwe or people who have who have actually spent time in Zimbabwe could provide accurate raw data for a study of the living conditions in Zimbabwe. If you input erroneous data, you can reach only erroneous conclusions.

Thus, the professor's 'statistically significant' conclusion was based upon faulty input from 18 and 19 year olds who had no experience of any kind with how married couples communicate. An absurd result was reached because absurd methods were applied to 'prove' a theory which in essence reflected nothing more than the opinions and biases of the professor conducting the study. Faulty methodology leads to not only wrong but oftentimes absurd conclusions. *The discipline of statistics does of course provide an accepted scientific approach to discovering correlations that lead to valid conclusions, but the type of data utilized and how it is inputted can nonetheless easily be manipulated to reach erroneous preconceived conclusions.*

Proving the Existence of Eccentricity

So, after reviewing how easily 'scientific' studies utilizing statistical correlations for proof can be manipulated, is there a sound and valid method of proving whether or not any person is eccentric? Valid proof of the existence of eccentricity in any individual can only be gleaned by:

Examining the biographical facts of any person's life to determine whether the facts of their life indicate the presence of all of the seven personality attributes of an eccentric person.

Let's illustrate the importance of this assertion through the use of a hypothetical example. While this example is hypothetical, the facts of this hypothetical scenario have likely occurred innumerable times.

A friend might suggest to you the next time you see him that you would enjoy meeting a friend of his, because he believes that his friend is interesting, witty, very smart, and fun to be around. But the opinions expressed to you by your friend of this third person are just that - opinions and not facts. Unlike psychological theory and speculation, which would be of little value in this hypothetical example, the only true test of whether you would find this potential new friend interesting, smart, witty and fun to be around is by actually spending time with him or her, because only then will you have a *factual basis* to rely upon in assessing the veracity of your friend's assertion that you would enjoy spending time with his friend.

Our introduction to the facts about people who are eccentric begins with a brief synopsis of the life of the world famous 16th century astronomer Galileo Galilei. The facts of his life will be viewed in the light of the seven personality attributes that define an individual as an eccentric person:

(1) Nonconforming attitude

(2) Creative

(3) Intense curiosity

(4) Idealistic

(5) Highly intelligent

(6) Opinionated

(7) Outspoken

Galileo is famous to this day for his 'heliocentric' astronomical discovery about the rotations of the earth in relation to the sun. When Galileo promulgated his radical idea that the earth revolved around the sun instead of the sun revolving around the earth, the prevailing belief taught by the Roman Catholic Church was that it was the sun that revolved around the earth. For defying the Catholic Church's doctrine, the Roman Catholic Inquisition tried Galileo for the crime of heresy. His life was spared by his being found not guilty of being a heretic but guilty of espousing heretical beliefs. Upon pain of death Galileo accepted his sentence of spending the rest of his life under house arrest.

Galileo's accomplishments contributed greatly to the advancement of civilization, and are mentioned to introduce the concept that eccentricity is frequently essential to the progress and advancement of civilization in any field. Galileo had a *nonconformist* and *outspokenly opinionated* spirit, a spirit that combined with his *curiosity* about the world that manifested itself in *creative* and *highly intelligent* solutions to the astronomical incongruities he observed. Those who are either afraid or unwilling to challenge the status quo as Galileo did can rarely if ever be the instruments of causing positive and beneficial changes to society. But was Galileo thanked for his nonconformist and outspoken ideas, hallmarks of an eccentric mind? Absolutely not! He was castigated, persecuted, called a lunatic and severely punished by the extant governing powers and entities of his day; in other words, instead of being recognized as the eccentric genius he was, in addition to being called a heretic by the Roman Catholic Church, Galileo was essentially deemed mentally deficient or *insane*.

Is Insanity The Same As Being Eccentric?

If a person is eccentric, it does not mean that a person is insane! But if you asked 100 people or 1,000 people the difference between being insane and being eccentric, many people would likely answer that: 'There is no difference.' Another typical response would frequently be this: 'Eccentric people are insane and insane people are eccentric. These two words essentially mean the same thing.' But eccentricity and insanity are two different and distinct concepts.

There are non-scientific definitions of eccentricity that are quite common. Among these erroneous definitions of the word 'eccentric' are explanations that a person is odd, crazy, or very unusual in a *bad* way, or out of his or her mind. You could probably add a few additional explanations of the word 'eccentric' that you have heard.

There are also legal definitions of insanity that exist in the United States and vary from state to state, but no state or federal statute defines eccentricity as a form of insanity. Perhaps the best definition I have ever heard of insanity I learned in my first year in law school at the then 7th ranked law school in the United States.

In a first year law school course entitled 'Criminal Law', students sat around an oval table with the professor at one end. This professor, in addition to earning a law degree from a top ten law school also had a PhD in psychology from another top ten university. He asked the class one by one what it meant to be legally insane.

Each student attempted their best to give the most erudite legal definition of insanity they could muster on such short notice, with each student, including me, seeming to try to outdo the rest of the class with the 'brilliance' of their definitions. When all of us had given our opinion on legal insanity, the professor sat silent for almost a minute. So, I raised my hand and asked him this question: "Professor, what do you think legal insanity means?" He replied, "It means you're crazy, you know, nuts, off your rocker." Naturally the class broke out in simultaneous laughter at such a simple definition given by a man with doctorates in both law and psychology.

The point of this true story is twofold: First, in the professor's definition of legal insanity given to the class after his comical definition, none of the attributes of eccentricity were mentioned. Incidentally, the DSM-V (Diagnostic & Statistical Manual of Mental Disorders, 5th Edition), utilized by psychiatrists and psychologists categorizes and provides an in depth explanation of every known mental disorder and it does *not* list eccentricity as a form of mental illness. I am acquainted with this psychiatric manual because after graduating from law school I practiced law for the better part of twenty years as a criminal defense attorney and close to half of my clients suffered from one or more mental disorders. Therefore, it was incumbent upon me as their attorney to be versant in the then current edition of the DSM (Diagnostic & Statistical Manual of Mental Disorders).

As an aside, I switched gears and became a pilot after practicing law. The reception I received as a pilot was quite a bit nicer than that received when I was a criminal defense attorney; a common saying then was that 'criminal defense lawyers are cut from the same cloth as their clients.' I have included this brief digression because it is illustrative of the tendency in human nature to hold misconceptions about things that we might not fully understand, whether it be criminal defense lawyers or eccentric people.

The second point relevant to this class discussion on legal insanity involved a related discourse dealing with how quick people are to label those that are eccentric as 'nuts', crazy', or 'off their rocker.' The alacrity with which some people are willing to denigrate eccentric people as possessed of some form of insanity is often done by people whose goal is to disparage the person they are mocking because they disagree with them on some key subject, such as a political or religious point of view, or as the French say, any *'au current'* issues being the current subject of debate in the country.

If an argument for any position has no more strength to it that one must resort to calling those who disagree with him or her 'crazy' or 'eccentric', that is a sad state of affairs. It also does nothing to help anyone be more respectful and tolerant.

A fairly recent example of this disparaging attitude occurred when the comedian Dave Chappelle, star of the highly rated cable show on Comedy Central entitled *'Chappelle's Show'*, in 2005 decided not to accept a $50 million contract offer to continue the series for three years. At the time the offer was made, the series was rated #33 in all categories of television series.

Dave instead made a trip to Africa, and as a result the media largely concluded that Mr. Chappelle had lost his mind. In a later television interview on the program *Inside the Actor's Studio*, he described with anguish how hurtful it was to go from being a top comedian, widely respected, to being derogated as simply insane. Sadly, it seems a part of human nature to, as the old saying goes, 'kick someone when they're down.' Chappelle is definitely eccentric in a wonderful way that brought laughter and joy to millions of viewers of his television show, but is by no means insane.

Chapter 2

THE ORIGIN OF AND CHANGES IN THE MEANING OF THE WORD ECCENTRIC

"All our words from loose using have lost their meaning."

Ernest Hemingway

The origin and history of any word is called *'etymology'*. Etymology can be quite boring, but at least it is not as boring as a similarly spelled word, 'entomology', which is the study of insects! Etymology reveals how a word first came into existence and the history and development of any word over time. In order to understand the present day usage of a word, *there is no better way to achieve that goal but by a very brief historical account of how the word 'eccentric' came into existence and how its meaning has evolved over time.*

This is a book about eccentricity and not a polemic of my own personal opinions on various subjects, even though my opinions are synonymous with fact...... but jesting aside, a brief digression to comment on Ernest Hemingway's observation about words is in my opinion useful because the deterioration of language skills today and the knowledge of words and their meaning is lamentable.

Simple and short laconic speech is often the best way to communicate, but not always, and this is especially true of non-fiction books such as this one. So called 'big words' have gradations of meaning that add clarity to the writer's intended meaning, especially on complex subjects. Oftentimes there is no way to express a thought or concept other than through the use of vocabulary that is usually not used in everyday conversation.

For example, countless modern day works of literature, history, philosophy, and many other subjects, even novels not regarded as great literary works, use words that are unfamiliar to many people. I have tried to whenever possible use simple words that are sufficiently capable of expressing correctly and clearly any thought, idea or concept discussed herein.

At the same time, I have not written this book using language at the level of members of the United States Congress, who speak and write at about a 10.6 grade level, down from 11.5 in 2005. By comparison, the U.S. Constitution was written at a 17.8 grade level, the Federalist Papers at a 17.1 grade level, and the United States Declaration of Independence at a 15.1 grade level. Ongoing scientific research on the subject of the trajectory since 2005 of the quality and complexity of the written word and speech used by members of the United States Congress reveals an overall steady decline post 2005. An adequate understanding of the meaning of the word *eccentricity* and its attributes is simply quite difficult to convey to the reader if written at the level of a present day 10th grader, which is a sophomore in high school. As Ernest Hemingway said, the loose use of words can cause words to lose their meaning, especially when the choice of vocabulary is simplified so much that it is inconsistent with the context in which a word is used and actually obscures the intended meaning of a sentence.

(1) ORIGIN AND HISTORY OF THE WORD 'ECCENTRIC'

'ECCENTRIC': The present day definition of *eccentric* originates from the Greek word *ekkentros,* which means "out of the center". The Greek word *exo means* "out of" and k*entron means* "center". The word 'eccentric' first appeared in English essays as a 'neologism' in the mid16th century. The word 'neologism' is simply a combination of the Greek word 'neo', which means 'new', and 'logos', which means 'word'. In the 16th century the word 'eccentric' was in use only as an astronomical term that meant a circle in which the earth or the sun deviates from its center.

By the late 17th century the definition of the word 'eccentric' evolved from the literal to the figurative when the word *eccentric* began to be used to describe strange, unconventional, or odd behavior. The first use of the word *eccentric* as a noun that was intended to describe a person who possesses and exhibits unconventional or odd qualities or behaviors didn't occur until the early 19th century, in 1832.

Back in the 1830s eccentricity first began to be applied to people as individuals and was commonly associated with a high level of intelligence, creativity, and originality of thought. Beginning in the early 1830s eccentric people were usually admired. But with the passage of time eccentric people were perceived in an uncomplimentary way. As people became more aware of the term *eccentric,* they started attaching very pejorative connotations to the word *eccentric* and to eccentric people.

Non-eccentric people often had little respect for eccentric people because they failed to comport themselves in a manner consistent with then prevailing values held by the culture and the society of their time. For the majority of people in society that were not eccentric, eccentric people 'upset the apple cart' of the security that non-eccentric people found in adhering to the values and modes of behavior that were regarded as socially acceptable. This was very understandable because behavior that is different and nonconformist can oftentimes be disconcerting.

English utilitarian thinker John Stuart Mill (Born May 20, 1806, Died May 8, 1873) was an English philosopher, a profound thinker, feminist, political economist, and civil servant who also had deeply held convictions about the value of being eccentric. He was an influential contributor to social theory, political theory, and economics. He has been called "the most influential English speaking philosopher of the nineteenth century".

Mill expressed his view on freedom by illustrating how an individual's drive to better their station, and the desire for self-improvement that is subsumed in the pursuit of bettering one's station in life, is in fact according to Mill the sole source of obtaining true freedom. He expounded and expatiated on his belief that true freedom can only prevail when an individual is able to attain self-improvement without impeding others in their efforts to do the same. Mill's linking of freedom and self-improvement has inspired many. By establishing that individual efforts to excel have worth, Mill was able to show that people could achieve self-improvement without harming others, or society at large.

This brief biographical synopsis of John Stuart Mill is included to show that his eloquent and definitive statement about the connection between eccentricity and the state of society came from a brilliant and well respected mind who was not shy about expressing his thoughts on the positive and beneficial value of eccentricity:

"The amount of eccentricity in a society has generally been proportional to the amount of genius, mental vigor, and moral courage which it contained,"
John Stuart Mill

Dame Edith Sitwell echoed Mill's sentiments by writing that eccentricity is *"often a kind of innocent pride"*. She also stated that geniuses and aristocrats are oftentimes called eccentrics because *"they are entirely unafraid of and uninfluenced by the opinions and vagaries of the crowd"*.

Eccentricity has also been associated with great wealth. The nexus between wealth and eccentricity is that if an eccentric person is successful in espousing and promoting their new and different ideas, wealth usually follows. I believe this reflects an unfortunate commentary on a common aspect of human nature, respecting the wealthy and disregarding the poor when what should be the defining judgment we make of any person, including eccentrics, is their character.

(2) PRESENT DAY DEFINITION OF THE TERM 'ECCENTRIC'

The root word 'eccentric' will shortly be defined according to various well known dictionaries, but first a caveat concerning the accuracy of dictionary definitions is needed. People usually consider a dictionary definition of a word reliable and true; in some cases the veracity of definitions found in dictionaries is almost sacrosanct even though different dictionaries often define the same word differently. Additionally, different dictionaries also frequently disagree as to the scope and breadth of the meaning of words, which is understandable because many words represent broad concepts that mean different things to different people. Dictionary definitions are also often incapable of revealing the complete truth about any given word because they are written by people with their own biases, experiences and perspectives on life who not infrequently and usually unintentionally infuse their definition of any given word with their own opinions.

For example, take the word 'tips'. 'Tips' could be defined as the ends of or the outermost point of an object, such as the tips of someone's toes or the tips of countless other objects. But tips can also mean advice given to someone, for example: 'Got any tips on any of the horses running in today's race?' Then again, 'tips' can also mean a monetary gratuity given to someone in appreciation of excellent service received; for example a diner at a restaurant telling his companion he never 'tips' less than 15%.

In Ecuador in South America, at the airport in Quito, Ecuador's capital city, I had an interesting experience that illustrated how an individual's personal experience with any given word can affect their perceptions of the meaning of a word. I was in Ecuador doing volunteer work for one month and was accompanied by six other volunteers who flew with me from the United States to assist me in the volunteer project I had planned and organized. Having been in Ecuador previously and having traveled around the world, I quickly became aware of the various local customs that exist in each country. When we landed in Quito, Ecuador and had made it through customs, I was the first member of our volunteer group to exit the airport and make my way to the sidewalk abutting the street where taxis were coming and going; we needed at least one, probably two taxis to take us to our hotel.

Glancing back at the exit door of the airport to make sure all the members of our volunteer group had cleared customs and were on their way to meet me, I saw one member of our group, Bob, who had never previously traveled outside of the United States, surrounded by about a dozen children that appeared to be approximately 7 to 17 years old. They were picking up Bob's luggage so that they could carry it to the sidewalk where I was standing hailing a taxi.

Bob shouted out to me from the midst of all the children and commented that these children were "the friendliest children I've ever seen." In fact, these children were known in Ecuador as *'touts'*, children who were steeped in poverty and were either homeless or suffering from malnutrition. First time travelers to a foreign country often make the mistake Bob did of bringing with him too much luggage. Bob had three suitcases with him that were now being carried by these friendly children to the curb where I was standing. The children set the luggage down, and Bob made the unfortunate mistake of repaying the children only with a heartfelt verbal 'thank you'. Then *'Me tips'* showed up.

The children were all crowding around Bob and each child was repeating to him "Me *tips, me tips."* Bob was bewildered; then the tallest of these children had soon made his way through the crowd of children and was now directly in front of Bob. He spoke to Bob the same refrain Bob had already heard from the rest of the touts: *'"Me tips, me tips".* Bob replied to this tallest child in the group of children who was now standing face to face with him: *"Me Bob, me Bob".* Lest the situation get out of control, I went up to Bob and explained to him that the children wanted to be compensated for carrying his luggage, and, that *'Me tips'* meant he should tip the children for carrying his luggage to the curb. So, Bob reached into his pocket and began handing out various Ecuadorian coins he obtained from one of the currency exchanges at the Quito airport.

The children then became visibly angry with Bob when he handed out his Ecuadorian coins to them and started kicking Bob in the shins and legs because all his Ecuadorian coins amounted to less than one U.S. dollar. I couldn't stop laughing about Bob's brief conversation with the tallest child there: *"Me tips, me tips"* he said to Bob, and Bob, thinking that *'tips'* was the child's name, replied *"Me Bob, me Bob."* I was able to defuse the situation by passing out to these Ecuadorian children paper Ecuadorian currency sufficient for them to be pleased. I explained to Bob that these children were *'touts'* who were poverty stricken and told Bob why they had carried his luggage. To this day I still remember Bob's encounter with *'Me tips'* outside the Quito airport and the word *'tips'* and still laugh about it. If the word *'tips'* has been colored by my experience that day with Bob and *"Me tips"*, I can only imagine how it has colored Bob's perception of the word! So, here are some definitions of the word 'eccentric', but as you read the following definitions bear in mind that they were written by people with their own set of experiences in life and biases that affect their conclusions regarding the meaning of any word:

ECCENTRIC:

The Merriam-Webster dictionary defines 'eccentric' thusly:

1. Deviating from an established or usual pattern or style;
2. Deviating from conventional or accepted usage or conduct especially in odd or whimsical ways;
3. Tending to act in strange or unusual ways;

A more recent and widely utilized dictionary, the internet dictionary, *Dictionary.com*, defines 'eccentric' as:

1. Deviating from the recognized or customary character, practice, etc.; irregular, erratic, peculiar, odd;
2. A person who has an unusual, peculiar, or odd personality, set of beliefs, or behavior pattern.

Eccentrics may or may not comprehend the standards for normal behavior in their culture. But history records that eccentric people are usually aware of customary standards for normal behavior and for social decorum. They are simply unconcerned by society's disapproval of their habits or beliefs. Many of history's most brilliant minds have displayed some unusual behaviors and habits. Some eccentrics are derogatorily dismissed as "cranks". Eccentric behavior has often been characterized as quirky or whimsical and can also be strange and disturbing to other people.

Many individuals previously considered merely eccentric, like aviation magnate Howard Hughes, have been retrospectively diagnosed as having suffered from mental disorders. But was he instead really an eccentric genius?

Other people may have eccentric tastes in clothes, or have eccentric hobbies or collections they pursue vigorously. They may have a pedantic and very precise manner of speaking, intermingled with inventive word-play. Many individuals may even manifest eccentricities consciously and deliberately in an attempt to differentiate themselves from societal norms or to enhance a sense of individuality and an inimitable identity. Fictional characters have often been associated with eccentricity, and accordingly some people deem it desirable to be associated with eccentric fictional character types because they are quite often very glamorous or heroic people. However, such efforts frequently fail due to the fact that an individual who believes he is eccentric when in fact he is not is usually dismissed by other people as someone who, sadly, is oftentimes lonely and just seeking attention and connection with other people.

(3) THE MISUSE TODAY OF THE TERM 'ECCENTRIC'

Unfortunately the pendulum of perceptions about eccentric people has shifted far away from the days of John Stuart Mill when eccentric people were much admired and valued. Today in modern western society eccentrics are usually only admired when their various accomplishments redound beneficially to the majority of those comprising a distinct culture. But absent notable positive success and achievement in their respective fields, eccentrics are usually disregarded, disparaged, and not infrequently castigated for their unconventional ideas and for the peculiarity of their personalities.

The net result of this change in perceptions about eccentric people is that the term 'eccentric' has shifted so far away from its true meaning that today the word has a pejorative connotation attached to it. This book endeavors to switch the pendulum of perception away from misconceptions about eccentricity and eccentric people through a circumspect, fact based examination of eccentricity and eccentric people.

Chapter 3

CHARACTERISTICS AND ATTRIBUTES OF ECCENTRIC PEOPLE

"Part of me would like to be accepted by all facets of society and not be this loudmouthed lunatic musician. But I cannot be what I am not."

John Lennon

A. THE VALUE OF BEING ECCENTRIC

(1) Eccentricity enables the pursuit of new ideas and modes of thinking that result in beneficial contributions to society.

(2) Eccentrics possess a singular ability to sort out confusion and crystallize the most important issues at hand, thereby unlocking the door to tremendous advancements in diverse fields that benefit society.

(3) With their unconventional ideas born of courage, eccentrics engender courage in others.

(4) Eccentrics possess a confident spirit that brings encouragement to those whose lives they touch.

B. CHARACTERISTICS AND ATTRIBUTES

In a groundbreaking research project done in the mid 1990s by David Weeks, a psychologist with a PhD in psychology, it is stated that people with a mental illness 'suffer' from their behavior while eccentrics are quite happy. His study also concluded that eccentrics are less prone to mental illness than everyone else. But the most important information concerning the lives of eccentric people that Weeks' study provided was that for the first time and through extensive personal interviews he identified specific attributes of eccentric people that serve as criteria for the existence of eccentricity in a person. Here is the list of Dr. Weeks' specific attributes of eccentric people:

1. Nonconformist

2. Happily obsessed with one or more hobbyhorses (usually five or six)

3. Strongly motivated by curiosity

4. Idealistic: he wants to make the world a better place and the people in it happier

5. Creative

6. Aware from early childhood that he is different

7. Single

8. Opinionated and outspoken; convinced he is right while others are out of step

9. Noncompetitive, not in need of reassurance or reinforcement from society

10. Unusual in his eating habits and living arrangements

11. Not particularly interested in the opinions or company of other people

12. Possessed of a mischievous sense of humor

13. Intelligent

14. Usually the eldest or an only child

15. A bad speller

Dr. David Weeks, with co-author Jamie James, wrote a book that was the final product of Dr. Weeks' research project on eccentricity. Dr. Weeks not only personally interviewed thousands of people claiming to be eccentrics, he also assessed the lives of some well known historical individuals with respect to the presence of eccentricity in their lives. Prior to his research, there was very little material available on eccentricity that was remotely of a scholarly nature or consistent with the principles of the scientific method of studying any subject. Weeks set forth the first modern day template, and an excellent one, for future study of this subject.

However, for reasons unknown to this author, the book that was the culmination of Dr. Weeks' research was sensationalized, largely taking Weeks' research out of the realm of accepted scientific research parameters by focusing instead predominately on the weirdest people he could find. That approach probably resulted in more book sales, but it also diminished his excellent research and sidestepped an analysis of the concept that valuable and beneficial contributions to society have been made by eccentrics.

Before probing into the specifics of the attributes of eccentric people that Dr. Weeks discovered, a 2012 self published book by Anie Knipping is worth mentioning, at least for its title, 'Eccentricity'. Unfortunately, her 'study' of eccentricity evinces very little understanding of her subject matter. While a very talented artist, her book was written as her senior year college project for her Bachelors of Fine Arts degree. Using her own life as the essential source of evidence, she equates eccentricity with mental illness in general and specifically with the mental disorder of social autism that she states she was afflicted with. 19th century thinkers such as John Stuart Mill had a much better understanding of eccentricity than Ms. Knipping possessed in 2012. Her book serves as an excellent example of how widely misunderstood eccentricity is unto the present day.

Anie Knipping's book on eccentricity also illustrates how easy it is to misconstrue your subject matter if you don't dig deeply into it or jump to conclusions too quickly. Had she studied the 200 years of history on eccentricity she would have likely been able to recognize that eccentricity is not the same as insanity nor can it be reduced to a distinct form of autism, social autism. Jumping to conclusions without thoroughly investigating your subject matter leads to misconceptions, misunderstandings, and of course results in erroneous conclusions being made of that subject matter. Something that happened to me on my first of many trips to India showed me the value of examining your subject matter very closely and the lack of worth of jumping to quick conclusions.

Around the world train stations in major cities all have in common the fact that the trains are actually indoors at the departure/arrival end of the train station. My wife and I had just boarded a train in New Delhi, the capital city of India, that was bound for the city of Chennai, then called Madras. I was seated on the right side of the train next to the window and my wife was sitting to my left. It took a minute or two for the train to clear the indoor portion of the terminal. As soon as the train was completely out of the train station and in the beautiful Indian sunlight, I looked out the window and saw the green grass about 150 yards to the right of the train filled to overflowing with Indian people. I watched them for a while, and then remarked to my wife, "Boy, these people really do love their families. Look at how they are all sitting out in the hot Indian sun just to say a last goodbye to their family or friends who are on our train."

My wife happened to glance out the window as the train turned closer to these people and asked me to take a second look at these people on the green grass to our right. I did, and then saw clearly that they were all defecating! The quick conclusion I had just made about what the Indian people on the grass were doing was totally false. Their presence near our train had nothing to do with saying goodbye to anyone on the train; they were on the grass to have a bowel movement. Due to a population of over 1 billion people and with poverty omnipresent throughout India, many Indians did not have a toilet in their dwelling place. So, the green grass was an absolutely splendid place for them to take a huge dump! The point is that just as I reached an erroneous conclusion because of my cursory glance at the people I could see from my train window, Ms. Knipping's book produced faulty conclusions and lacks merit because she failed to closely and thoroughly examine her subject matter, eccentricity.

Turning our attention back to Dr. Weeks mid 1990s book on eccentricity and how he sensationalized his findings, one of the most prominent eccentrics he utilizes for 'proof' was Joshua Abraham Norton, who in the mid19th century in San Francisco, California proclaimed himself to be and actually believed he was "Emperor of the United States and Mexico". Norton even had his own paper currency printed with his likeness on the bills! Rather than serving as an example of an eccentric individual, Norton was unquestionably suffering from some form of mental illness.

In fact, in reading Dr. Weeks' book, I often wondered whether I was reading a scientific psychological study of eccentrics and the attributes they held in common, or one of the many comic book magazines popular in the 20th century such as 'Strange Tales! Notwithstanding, Dr. Weeks' template of identifying eccentrics through common denominators in the lives of the eccentrics he studied was invaluable. As to the reason why his book veered off into the sensational and away from a fact based scientific study, my hunch is that the author's publisher compelled Dr. Weeks to make his book more sensationalist in order to sell more books. While my hunch may or may not be correct, citing people like the self proclaimed 'Emperor of the United States and Mexico', Joshua Abraham Norton, as legitimate examples of an eccentric person devalued and debased the very significant contribution made by Dr. David

Weeks in identifying the common denominators he believed were present in the lives of eccentrics.

Dr. David Weeks and co-author Jamie James, in my opinion, took another wrong turn in their study of eccentrics by deeming, for example, that the attribute eccentrics possess of being creative was on the same plane as their assertion that being single is an attribute of eccentrics. Another example was their equating being a bad speller of equal import as being highly intelligent.

According to David Weeks' study of eccentrics, the fifteen attributes he identified differentiate a healthy eccentric person from a normal person or someone who has a mental illness. This book is not in agreement that there are fifteen distinctive attributes that distinguish an eccentric person. The reasons for rejecting all but seven of these aforementioned fifteen attributes will be examined in further detail, but first let's take note of some other examples of eccentric people according to Dr. Weeks. He includes some exceptions from the examples of people like Joshua Abraham Norton by utilizing as examples of eccentric people Beethoven and Albert Einstein, but the majority of the people Dr. Weeks identified as eccentrics are in the mold of Joshua Abraham Norton. For example, Darla Shaw, is described thusly:

> *Another eccentric in our study, Darla Shaw, from western Connecticut, exhibits what might be called global eccentricity: she leads every aspect of her life in a non-conforming way. She believes that it's immoral to throw anything away, so she still owns everything she has ever purchased or been given. In addition to vast amounts of what most people would consider to be ordinary garbage, she owns a good stock of theatrical costumes, a life-sized Santa on skis, a paper-mache mermaid, a brace of stuffed alligators, and a portable shower that doubles as a telephone booth. Darla's hoard of earthly possessions finally grew to such vast proportions that she bought an abandoned opera house in order to have room for everything.*

Darla Shaw would have been more accurately described as a hoarder and likely suffering from some form of mental illness; instead, she was classified as an eccentric person. One more example from Dr. David Weeks book should be sufficient to illustrate the types of people his research deemed eccentric:

Here is an account from one eccentric, a twenty-five year old man named Peter, about the construction of his alternative reality: I have produced a fictitious Secondary World in response to living in the real one. This Secondary World does not set out to transport its inventor to a time or place that is far removed from the frightening realities of contemporary techno-society by conjuring up the conventional elements of myth. Rather, it is a place I model firmly on present world realities, a place where reflected versions of elements of the real world are carefully exaggerated, so that by imagining them as if they were real, their impact on me would be greater. And, this Secondary World serves me by interpreting and predicting events in the real one.

The previous comments of Darla Shaw and Peter are excellent examples of the mentally ill, but not of true eccentrics. And, what on earth does being a bad speller or noncompetitive, or being unusual in one's eating habits or living arrangements, or being single or an eldest child, have to do with eccentricity? And where is the key attribute integral to eccentricity, idealism, to be found in the lives of Darla Shaw and Peter?

The psychologist Dr. Weeks also states that being a nonconformist was in his opinion a primary attribute of an eccentric. But crazy people are often nonconformists as well and they aren't eccentric just because they are nonconformists. The absence of idealism, intelligence, creativity or outspokenness found in the examples Dr. Weeks used for proof of eccentricity instead provides more convincing proof of their possessing a mental illness, as in the case of the "Emperor" of the United States and Mexico, Joshua Abraham Norton. As for positive contributions to the world made by people he cites in his book as eccentrics, most of his examples of people he deemed eccentric made no positive contributions to society. Dr. Weeks' book is dominated by examples of people he deemed eccentric that were in fact not eccentric but were suffering from one or more mental disorders. Psychological studies of eccentricity can contribute much to understanding eccentric people, but the very few that exist are frequently little more than flawed sensationalized psychological babble.

Psychological theories are just that - theories which sometimes are proven true and sometimes false. But the lives eccentric people lived are not speculative theories but fact and are far more substantive and compelling indicia of truth and veracity than theories alone.

The seven attributes of eccentricity are listed below, and the remaining four attributes, which appear below the line, occur frequently in eccentric people but their inclusion herein as a necessary qualifier for an individual to be eccentric is not essential. By the way, having to turn to a table every time a significant aspect of a book is mentioned can be tedious; therefore the following seven attributes possessed by all eccentric people will be listed for your convenience whenever referred to:

(1) Nonconforming attitude

(2) Creative

(3) Intense curiosity

(4) Idealistic

(5) Highly intelligent

(6) Opinionated

(7) Outspoken

---

* Sometimes not interested in the opinions or company of other people
  • Mischievous sense of humor
* Knew in early childhood that he or she was different from others
  • Happy obsession with a hobby or hobbies

Before proceeding further, while these seven attributes are words whose meaning is probably familiar to everyone, because these attributes are an inextricable part of eccentric people and must all be present to satisfy the criteria for an eccentric person, a definition of each attribute from the *Oxford English Dictionary* is given, with the cautionary prefatory remarks mentioned earlier that dictionary definitions are incapable of revealing the complete truth about the meaning of any given word because dictionary definitions are written by people with their own experiences and biases who, intentionally or unintentionally, inevitably infuse their definitions with their own beliefs and perspectives. As was also mentioned earlier, additional proof of the fact that dictionary definitions are all colored to some extent with the bias of the person writing a dictionary definition can be seen by the fact that different dictionaries often define the same word differently.

1. Nonconforming attitude (nonconformist)

nonconformist - A person who does not conform to prevailing ideas or established practice.

2. Creative

creative - Relating to or involving the use of imagination or original ideas to create something.

3. Intense curiosity

intense - Of extreme force, degree or strength. _curiosity_ - A strong desire to know or learn something.

4. Idealistic

idealistic (idealism) - The belief that your ideals can be achieved, often when this does not seem likely to others. {From Cambridge University English Dictionary}. Note: Some editions of the Oxford English Dictionary state that an idealistic person pursues their ideals "unrealistically". If this definition was actually true, idealism would be little more than a myth of no value to anyone and would belie the nobility of purpose intrinsic to the beliefs of idealists, and more importantly, the very concept of idealism would be emasculated of its true purpose. The most accurate definition of 'idealistic' is from dictionary.com: "The cherishing or pursuit of high or noble principles, purposes, goals, etc."

5. Highly intelligent

intelligent [or smart] - Having a high level of ability to vary [a person's] state or action in response to varying situations and past experience.

6. Opinionated

opinionated - Assertively dogmatic in one's views.

dogmatic - Inclined to assert principles or opinions as incontrovertibly true. _Note:_ This definition, like the Oxford English Dictionary definition of 'idealistic', is a superb example of personal bias or opinions of the person writing the definition confusing the true meaning of a word. Most people who are opinionated believe their opinion is correct or they wouldn't hold it, but at the same time they also acknowledge that any opinion, including their own, could be inaccurate and that their opinion is not necessarily "in-

controvertibly true" and they are therefore wiling to modify or change their opinion when facts persuade them that their opinion is incorrect.

7. **Outspoken**

outspoken - *Frank in stating one's opinions.*

When the word **'eccentric'** is used to disparage a person to the point that their personal or professional reputation is damaged beyond repair, society loses some of its most innovative and creative people because it is eccentric individuals who have spawned some of the greatest and best social, political, religious, artistic, scientific and other advancements in culture and society that benefit nearly everyone.

There also exists a deleterious risk in equating eccentricity with insanity and this danger should be quite obvious: Once a person believes that being eccentric is the same as a person being insane, eccentrics in society will receive the same treatment the insane receive. People who are insane are invariably - depending on the person's view of the insane - pitied, mocked, considered an outcast incapable of making a positive contribution to society, sought to be medically healed of their insanity, and, the gamut of ways people view the insane is so vast that they would take up several pages just to categorize.

Suffice it to say that whether on the one end of the spectrum one views the insane as deficient human beings who need help or one believes the insane to be worthy of little more than derision and contempt, the end result is the same: The insane are deemed to be in some manner deficient and accordingly never really considered as individuals with a beneficial contribution to make to society or the lives of people close to them. And, if eccentrics are judged insane, they are treated likewise.

Yet, throughout recorded history, innovations in every major field of endeavor, including but not limited to science, literature, music, art, and government saw great advancements and breakthroughs in these various disciplines rarely made by people who accepted the status quo of their time and refused to challenge it. Think about it from the vantage point of simple logic and the seven attributes of eccentric people, using the heliocentric views of Galileo as an example, and ask yourself whether Galileo could have ever made his bold pronouncement that the earth revolved around the sun had he *not* possessed all of the following attributes of an eccentric person:

(1) Nonconforming Attitude

(2) Creative

(3) Intense Curiosity

(4) Idealistic

(5) Highly intelligent

(6) Opinionated

(7) Outspoken

The greatest damage done by disparaging eccentric people, whether they are notable world figures of renown or your neighbor down the street or a family member is simple: Once we have chosen to dismiss the value of a man or woman simply because of their eccentricity, we can see them in no other light but as inferior people. And, once we have judged someone inferior to ourselves, it becomes impossible for us to look beyond the eccentricities of the person with the result that all the contributions that they could have made to the world, their community, or even their family are not only never made, it is never even deemed possible that such an eccentric person could have an important idea to share.

In essence, it is a reasonable conclusion to state that once people conclude that someone is eccentric and believes that eccentrics are lesser people or that eccentricity is akin to insanity, they would no longer look to an eccentric person for wisdom or guidance or as a potential source of solving a problem of their own any more than human beings would seek knowledge or wisdom or advice from a monkey!

But if a host of contributions to the advancement of civilization have been made by eccentrics, it begs the question of why anyone would summarily dismiss the value of an eccentric person simply because they are eccentric. One doesn't need to be a trained psychiatrist to realize that the harmful emotions that have plagued humanity since the beginning of time are usually the culprit: jealousy, ignorance, envy, a need to establish a person's own self worth by demeaning another person, and that residue of the worst kind of evil that ever existed, hatred of a person because they are different than we are. Whether we disparage a person because their skin color is different than ours or because their political views are different than ours or because they are eccentric, the fertile bedding ground for hatred of another human being is spawned.

Think of the cultural loss to western society if Elvis Presley, who possessed all of the seven attributes of an eccentric person, had never been allowed to appear on television because his sexually suggestive physical gyrations and radically different music was deemed unacceptable because it was outside of the parameters of then prevailing musical and cultural norms and standards. If the widespread condemnation of Elvis Presley had succeeded in thwarting his musical career, Rock 'n Roll would quite possibly never have been born, and The Beatles might have never changed the face of pop music forever.

Music is a powerful unseen force that has inspired and comforted people worldwide through the expressiveness of its musical artists. If we reject people solely on their eccentricity or reject musical innovations simply because they don't conform to then prevailing standards for what is deemed acceptable at any given point in time, the end result is the same: progress is impeded or thwarted altogether.

Elvis Presley is of course not alone in the music world. The Beatles were also quite nonconforming, outspoken, opinionated, highly intelligent, curious, and possessed a level of creativity that is staggering in its depth and scope. Although we now accept classical music, jazz, the blues, and artists like Elvis Presley and The Beatles as part of mainstream culture, in their day most new forms of music were initially met with opposition and even condemnation. When we realize that eccentric people have often been our favorite musical artists, then perhaps a book on the value of eccentric people is more relevant to our own lives than we might have initially thought.

Chapter 4

COURAGE: THE BINDING THREAD OF ECCENTRIC INDIVIDUALS

"It is not because things are difficult that we do not dare;
It is because we do not dare that they are difficult."

Seneca

"Be daring, be different, be impractical; be anything that will assert integrity of purpose and imaginative vision against the play-it-safers, the creatures of the commonplace, the slaves of the ordinary."

Sir Cecil Beaton

Courage has always been and remains the common denominator and thread that binds eccentric individuals. Though all courageous people are not eccentric, with few exceptions all eccentrics have an inner courage. For example, in the field of statistics, denying the intrinsic courage of eccentrics would be referred to as an 'outlier', i.e., a viewpoint at odds with the overwhelming majority of statistical correlations proving cause and effect of any given theorem.

An example familiar to most people would be polls in U.S. presidential election primaries for the Republican or Democrat nomination. Specifically, if for example nine such presidential polls revealed a clear preference for candidate 'A' to win a given state's presidential primary by a significant margin over other contenders, and a lone tenth poll stated an opposing preference for candidate 'B', the tenth poll that directly contradicts the nine other polls favoring candidate 'A' and predicts victory by candidate 'B' would be an outlier.

Think of *courage* as the powerhouse or engine that *enables the expression of eccentric ideas*, analogous to the jet engines that power Boeing and Airbus jet airplanes that transport people to every part of the globe. Every eccentric person examined in this book was indisputably a courageous person in varying ways depending on the differing opposition or danger each one faced in their own respective lives.

The meaning of the word *'courage'* is pretty much universally understood around the world. A dictionary endeavors to define the exact meaning of a word, but dictionary definitions are incapable of revealing the complete truth about any given word because, as stated previously, they are written by people with their own biases. The word *'courage'* is a good example of how easily bias can creep into a definition, because what are acts of courage to one person are often acts of stupidity or irrational behavior to another. So, recognizing the limitations inherent in ascertaining the exact meaning of a word, according to the *Oxford English Dictionary* the definition of *'courage'* is:

courage

1. *Bravery;*
2. *The ability to do something that frightens one;*
3. *Standing for one's convictions and acting on one's beliefs despite danger or disapproval;*
4. *Strength in the face of pain or grief;*

According to Dictionary.com, *courage* is defined as:

1. *The quality of mind or spirit that enables a person to face difficulty, danger, pain, etc., without fear; bravery;*
2. *Having the courage to act in accordance with one's beliefs, especially in spite of criticism;*

Now, let's compare what courage is with respect to four of the seven attributes of eccentric people and ask yourself this question: Does the expression of these attributes require courage?

(1) Nonconforming Attitude

(4) Idealistic

(6) Opinionated

(7) Outspoken

It is improbable for a person to posses and express the above four attributes of eccentric people absent courage. A nonconforming attitude expressed to other people is not spoken absent risk to the courageous, nonconforming person willing to speak their mind. If you are willing to express strong opinions to other people, you may also face not only rejection but the prospect that the person or persons you are expressing your opinions to does not share them and will not only disapprove, but cause you to face danger either of an economic, physical, social, or other type. The same risks apply to being outspoken and idealistic.

It is inimical to the very nature of eccentricity for an eccentric person to lack a significant measure of courage because their achievements and accomplishments in life were almost always made in the face of much opposition and even fervent hostility to either them, their ideas, or both. It is relatively easy to admire the courage of an American soldier in the American Revolutionary War who willingly gave his life for his country, just as it is easy to admire the courageous British, American, French and Allied troops who willingly sacrificed their own lives to free the world of Adolph Hitler's Nazi despotism and inhuman brutality.

The grace and fortitude of the Jewish holocaust victims and survivors refusing to yield the only thing left to them, their belief in God and their values of love and their abhorrence of hatred, were without question courageous. The obscure father who sacrifices his own life to throw his young child off of train tracks she was innocently playing on and out of the way of an onrushing train, all the while knowing that it would cost him his own life under the unrelenting wheels of the powerful locomotive, is easily understood by anyone.

Likewise, the heroic first responders who fearlessly and without hesitation sacrificed their own lives to save people trapped in the Twin Towers of New York City on September 11, 2001 when they were completely destroyed by terrorists hijacking and flying airplanes into the two massive buildings is indisputable and easily recognized. Countless other examples of courageous acts throughout the history of mankind could be documented here as well. But the courage of an eccentric person is not so easily perceived much less recognized by others except retrospectively, when their contributions to society were documented facts capable of being read in history books.

Eccentric individuals buck prevailing trends and norms. To stand alone against prevailing societal norms or even the belief systems of the circle of friends of a person simply is impossible absent the presence of a courageous spirit. Courage is at the very heart and soul of every eccentric person and the one underlying ingredient that must be present for the seven attributes of eccentric people to even exist. But is that courageous spirit admired or valued in the moment of its expression? Regrettably, though there are notable exceptions such as the widely admired eccentric British prime minister during World War II, Winston Churchill, usually it is rarely the case that the courage of eccentric people is clearly recognized in the moment of its expression.

Courage has always been and remains the common denominator and thread, the inner intrinsic force that eccentric individuals possess. Carrying this truth further, if we universally admire courageous people, once we understand the great courage required to express one's eccentric beliefs or ideas, perforce rather than being looked down upon or mocked or disparaged, eccentric individuals should be admired for their courage - because it is courage that fuels their nonconforming and outspoken beliefs and ideas.

Chapter 5

HISTORICAL ECCENTRICITY: 16th CENTURY TO 19th CENTURY

"Only as you do know yourself can your brain serve you as a sharp and efficient tool. Know your own failings, passions, and prejudices so you can separate them from what you see."

Bernard Baruch

T hough deemed unconventional, peculiar and even radical in their extant milieu, the engines of profound positive changes in society have often been eccentrics. History is replete with examples illustrating that forward movement in society is led by those considered - in the time of the advent of the exposition of their new ideas - radical and eccentric for their time. Chapters 6 through 9 will examine four people who are credited with making enormous contributions to society yet were also eccentric:

(1) Martin Luther

(2) Vincent van Gogh

(3) Benjamin Franklin

(4) Lord Byron

Before looking into the lives of any of these eccentric people, it is worth noting that there are many more equally notable and successful eccentrics who could have been included in this book. The choice of narrowing the list down to twelve eccentric individuals was based upon three criteria:

1. Their lives must be a matter of historical record that is verifiable;
2. Their achievements in life must have benefited society;
3. They must collectively represent eccentric people from a sufficiently diverse variety of fields and time periods so that it can be easily seen that eccentric people are an indispensable and vital force behind positive innovations and beneficial contributions made to society.

Many other eccentric people who made notable contributions to the world they lived in, for example Steve Jobs, have not been included because a balance needed to be struck between having too few people included to provide a credible basis for the contention that eccentric people have great value while on the other hand avoiding the inclusion of so many eccentrics that an adequate summary of the facts of their lives would not be possible without this book totaling several thousand pages.

The focus herein is the value of being eccentric. Accordingly, each historical figure's life is viewed from the lens of the nexus between their lives and the part that eccentricity played in their respective achievements and contributions to society.

With respect to the thesis of this book, anyone who believes in the validity of their perspective on a given subject of necessity makes no apology for their point of view. Esteemed historians who write scholarly biographies express their own opinions regarding the person they have chosen to write a book about, including their admiration or lack thereof for the subject of their biography. I admire the idealism, courage, and nonconformist perspectives of the eccentric people you will read about in this book, individuals who advanced the progress of mankind through their inner fuel of society's secret sauce, eccentricity. Notwithstanding, the biographical synopses of the lives of the people examined in this book are completely factual and have not been skewed or shaded in any way.

Integral to my motivation in writing this book is the belief that eccentric people constitute an innumerable amount of people around the globe and that a better understanding of the nature of eccentricity would foster not only a greater understanding of eccentric people but also a greater understanding of people that are in any way different than we are. Let's briefly extrapolate from the value of being tolerant and understanding of eccentric people to this broader context, tolerance and understanding of people who *are in any way different than we are.*

Poets and songwriters possess a unique ability to express profound ideas in a pithy fashion, as was displayed in the 1982 song written and recorded by Paul McCartney entitled *Ebony And Ivory*, which spent seven weeks at #1 in the Billboard rankings in the year of its release. The central theme of the song was a plea for racial harmony. Trading vocals with African American musician Stevie Wonder on the record, the main theme of the song was expressed through the metaphor of piano keys being black and white, a clever approach to advocating for racial harmony when McCartney wrote: *Ebony and ivory live together in perfect harmony on my piano keyboard, oh Lord, why can't we?* Song lyrics are often poetry, and poets are gifted in their ability to express truth on any given theme from multiple angles. All right, you might say, but what does this song have to do with eccentricity? Read on.

In *Ebony & Ivory,* McCartney's lyrics drove home his belief in racial harmony, but there is also a second powerful theme to the song: The recognition that everyone is imperfect, when he wrote: *There is good and bad in everyone. We learn to live, learn to give each other what we need to survive, together alive.* If we can understand that there is good and bad in people of all skin colors then we won't condemn people solely on the basis of the color of their skin. *And if people should not be disparaged and rejected solely because of the color of their skin, neither should any person who is eccentric be denigrated and scorned just because they are eccentric.* Remember, there is good and bad in everyone, including eccentrics and non-eccentrics. The truth that there is good and bad in every person was eloquently summarized in the quotation at the beginning of this chapter:

"Only as you do know yourself can your brain serve you as a sharp and efficient tool. Know your own failings, passions, and prejudices so you can separate them from what you see."

Bernard Baruch

The broad theme of McCartney's song *is being tolerant and understanding of people that are different than we are. Eccentric people are different than the majority of the population.* If we stay cognizant of our own prejudices then we can keep an open mind towards everyone, including eccentric people. When a person recognizes these truths, he or she fosters a spirit of understanding that sprouts up like a beautiful flower from the earth.

It is quite unlikely that eccentric people had anything to do with the motivation behind McCartney's lyrics to *Ebony & Ivory,* but its extension to eccentricity through the application of principles of logical reasoning is patent. The lyrical message of the song was so powerful, as was its beautiful melody and arrangement, that today it is ranked #69 on Billboard's Hot 100 chart. As wise people know that they can learn something from a seven year old child, wise souls also realize that they can learn from a simple pop music song. If we are not haughty and do not dismiss the fact that we can learn from a young child or a pop song, then humility grows; and when humility grows, the ability to keep an open mind increases and expands — and extends even to the *'strange'* notion that eccentric people should not be rejected, dismissed, disparaged or denigrated solely by virtue of their being eccentric.

As was stated earlier the biographical information of the twelve people utilized in this book is of necessity limited because it would easily require thousands of pages to provide more than biographical synopses of their lives, and my purpose is not to write yet another biography of these well known individuals but to relate the historical facts of their lives to their eccentricity. The *Bibliography* of this book contains some of the best biographies of the twelve people that are the subject of this book should you be inclined to learn more about the fascinating lives they led.

Chapter 6

MARTIN LUTHER

*"You are not only responsible for what you say,
but also for what you do not say."*

Martin Luther

Martin Luther, (Born November 10, 1483, Died February 18, 1546) early in his career and before becoming the founding and seminal figure behind the Protestant Reformation was a German professor of theology, a monk, and a priest. After rejecting the teachings of the Catholic Church, Luther forsook his life as a monk and a priest but became an even more perspicacious theologian and a prolific writer who used his pen to express his vehement opposition to the papacy and the fundamental doctrines of the Catholic Church. He was also an accomplished musician, a composer of hymns, and a multi-linguist. Martin Luther is most remembered today as the leading figure and driving force of the Protestant Reformation.

After profound inner turmoil, Luther rejected several significant teachings and practices of the Late Medieval Catholic Church. He strongly disputed the claim that freedom from God's punishment for sin could be purchased with money. He proposed an academic discussion of the power and usefulness of indulgences in his famous *Ninety-Five Theses* of 1517 that he nailed to the church door in Wittenberg.

During the decade in which Luther was born Pope Sixtus IV had declared that the efficacy of indulgences extended to purgatory for the benefit of the living and the dead alike. Indulgences gave partial remission of the punishment that is still due to God for a sin or sins. The method by which the Catholic Pope offered relief from purgatory was a written document called a *'Bull of Indulgence'*. In the case of the living there was no assurance of avoiding purgatory entirely because God alone knew the full extent of unexpiated guilt and the consequent length of the sentence, but the Church could tell anyone to the year and the day by how much the term could be reduced, whatever it was. And in the case of those already dead and in purgatory, the sum of whose wickedness was complete and known, an immediate release could be offered. Some of these Bulls of Indulgences went even further and applied not merely to reduction of penalty but even to the forgiveness of sins. They offered a plenary remission and reconciliation with God. Unfortunately these Bulls of Indulgence were not given away for free by the Pope but were sold for a price, and that price was always the payment of money to the Catholic Church.

Originally a devout and deeply devoted son of the Catholic Church, Martin Luther eventually decimated the structure of medieval Catholicism. Luther had a great affinity for those living in poverty, which led to his eventually equating the popes with Antichrist because the Pope made the poor pay the Catholic Church money for indulgences while the Pope himself lived in luxury and splendor as one of the wealthiest men in Europe. Luther also lived in an era when incipient nationalism was growing with fervor at the same time the Reformation contributed to the destruction of the existing religious order. Regardless of the effects that nationalism had on religious reform, the egregious and audacious chicanery of the pope charging money for indulgences was so outrageous that indulgences standing alone would probably have brought forth the Reformation.

Nationalism was not the only non-religious occurrence that converged on the religious Reformation. Another intersecting phenomena was the Renaissance, a mode of thought based essentially on humanism. The Renaissance was in essence an all encompassing attitude to life that was founded upon the principle and perspective that the main focus of mankind should be men. The Renaissance in a different way stood as an opposing force to popery and its abusive practices, especially the selling of indulgences, even though it didn't mount such an intense and virulent opposition to the pope as Luther did. The reason that Renaissance adherents never evolved into as passionate and proactive opponents of the Catholic Church as Luther did was because the popes of the Renaissance period became some of the most prominent patrons of the Renaissance. These popes viewed the Renaissance as an apropos marriage between the classical world and the Christianity already espoused by St. Augustine.

The concept of a *Renaissance Man* can best be described in principle as the humanist belief that the main focus of mankind should be man. The practical implementation of this belief was a man who was accomplished in multiple fields, including but not limited to exploration, science, art, music, politics and the languages and literature of antiquity. But the

Renaissance was at the same time still a threat to the Catholic Church because being centered on man and not religion, the selling of indulgences was antithetical to the principles of the Renaissance.

Luther's fierce opposition to indulgences resulted in his vehement persecution by the Catholic Church. The person selling the indulgences in Germany in Martin Luther's day was a man named Tetzel. Luther's outspoken, opinionated spirit and courage were on full display in 1517 when he wrote a letter to a representative of the Catholic Church, a man named Prierias. Luther was replying to the ever increasing persecution he faced from the Catholic Church:

> "I am sorry now that I despised Tetzel. Ridiculous as he was, he was more acute than you. You cite no Scripture. You give no reasons. Like an insidious devil you pervert the Scriptures. You say that the Church consists virtually in the pope. What abominations will you not have to regard as the deeds of the Church? Look at the ghastly shedding of blood by Julius II. Look at the outrageous tyranny of Boniface VIII, who as the proverb says, 'came in as a wolf, reigned as a lion, and died as a dog.'"

The above excerpt of Martin Luther in his own words reveals an individual who clearly was a vigorously outspoken nonconformist and a very creative and curious thinker who expressed himself with intellectual acumen as a writer. Luther also possessed a high level of intelligence capable of discerning falsehoods masquerading as truth. The risks he took in life by standing boldly for his beliefs were born of a very idealistic nature. Luther was offended at the practice of selling indulgences not only from a theological perspective but because he genuinely felt for the common people, most of them poor, who were victimized by indulgences. Luther wanted to free them of the costly burden of paying money to the Catholic Church for a promise predicated upon a lie. He was a man unafraid of challenging the religious status quo. Luther was also intensely curious throughout his lifetime, especially with respect to the validity of then extant theological beliefs. This excerpt from Luther's life reveals an individual who was possessed of the full panoply of eccentric attributes:

(1) Nonconforming attitude

(2) Creative

(3) Intense curiosity

(4) Idealistic

(5) Highly intelligent

(6) Opinionated

(7) Outspoken

When Luther refused to retract all of his writings at the demands of Pope Leo X in 1520 and the Holy Roman Emperor Charles V at the Diet of Worms in 1521, the response by the Pope and Charles V was unyielding. He was condemned as an outlaw by the Emperor and excommunicated by the Pope. The penalty Luther faced as a result was death. In standing boldly for his convictions, Luther unwaveringly displayed a nonconformist, outspoken, idealistic spirit infused with courage.

Luther taught that salvation and subsequently eternal life is not earned by good deeds but is received only as a free gift of God's Grace through faith in Jesus Christ as redeemer from sin. His theology challenged the authority and office of the Pope by teaching that the Bible is the sole source of divinely revealed knowledge from God and opposed sacerdotalism by considering all baptized Christians to be a holy priesthood. Martin Luther's rhetoric condemning the papacy was challenged by some not on its merits or on any other substantive basis but rather as the outspoken outbursts of a man who was enamored of his own opinions. Such criticism was patently ridiculous because opinions are the gateway to the maturation of strong beliefs on any subject.

Martin Luther's teachings soon gained a widespread following. Those who made the decision to identify themselves with Luther's theology and embrace Luther's teachings began to be called *Lutherans*, even though Luther disliked his followers being called Lutherans and taught them that the terms *Christian* or *Evangelical* best described those who had freed themselves from the shackles of the bloody tyranny and avarice of the medieval Roman Catholic Church.

Martin Luther's intellect was on par with the greatest minds history has known. His mental prowess and capacity for deep conceptual thought are mirrored throughout his writings. Proof of Luther's deep intellect is revealed not only through his words but through the effect his words had on initiating and establishing the greatest reformation of Christianity the world had hitherto seen.

Luther acted upon his beliefs not only in the exposition and defense of his spiritual revelations but through actions that moved him to translate the Bible into the vernacular of the people (German instead of Latin), making it more accessible, which had a tremendous impact on the church and German culture. In addition to the German language Bible translation made by Luther from original Hebrew and Greek texts that led to the development of a standard version of the German language Bible, his German translation served as a model and inspiration for the writing of an English translation, the Tyndale Bible. His hymns contributed immensely to the development of worship in church through music and hymns, a practice foreign to the Catholic Church.

Once the Reformation had taken hold in Germany, Luther was not the first Protestant clergyman to marry but he was the first Protestant leader to teach that marriage was not proscribed by the Bible. It was not until he was 42 that he finally decided he was ready for marriage himself. His marriage to Katherine von Bora did however, because of Luther's stature as the leader of the Reformation, serve as a paradigm for marriage by the clergy.

Martin Luther's eccentricity abounds not only in his nonconformist 95 Theses nailed to the church door in Wittenberg, Germany but throughout his voluminous writings, which in present day book form amount to approximately 20 thick bound volumes, give or take a few depending on the book publisher. A prolific writer, Luther used humor combined with plain common sense written in the language of the German speaking people to point out medieval papal absurdities.

Luther was courageously outspoken, both verbally and through his voluminous writings. In several letters and longer essays Luther wrote that it was absurd and utterly ridiculous for the pope of Rome to charge money to the poorest of peasants to free their loved ones from purgatory into the bliss of heaven. Reading Luther's writings left this writer cackling away at the brilliant logical mind and humorous spirit of Luther when he rhetorically asked the Pope why, if he was the Vicar of Christ as he claimed to be, he chose not to follow the example of Christ in never charging a penny for the good deeds and miracles credited to Jesus in the Bible but instead passionately overthrew the tables of the merchants who used the temple to sell their religious wares at a profit.

On one occasion while in Saxony with monks observing, Luther threw his inkstand at a grinning image of Satan, resulting in said monks regarding Martin Luther as quite odd indeed! However, Luther was not known to exhibit a large pattern of such eccentric behavior that wasn't theologically or intellectually based.

This stresses an important point, that eccentrics sometimes but not always find their eccentricity marked by infrequent rather than habitual or oft occurring manifestations of the kind of quirkiness exhibited when Luther threw his inkstand at an image of Satan. Such displays of eccentric behavior are far more easily discerned by other people as acts of an eccentric mind than are some of the seven attributes of eccentric people, such as being curious, nonconforming, creative, or highly intelligent. In other words, as is recounted in the section on Albert Einstein later on in this book, you don't have to commit obviously eccentric acts like Einstein did in smoking half smoked cigarette butts he picked up off the street in order to be eccentric.

Luther's intense curiosity and gargantuan and brilliant intellect was also reflected through Luther being regarded as a *Renaissance Man* even though Luther didn't subscribe to the humanist doctrine of the Renaissance. As was mentioned earlier the term *Renaissance Man* means a person talented in multiple different fields. The fact that Martin Luther was a *Renaissance Man* is attested to by Luther being a very accomplished lute (a predecessor to the guitar) musician, a composer of hymns, a preacher, and of course an astute and renowned theologian who wrote numerous books, essays and treatises. He was also a multi-linguist fluent in the German, Latin, Greek and Hebrew languages. Like anyone Martin Luther had his flaws and foibles. They included being at times short tempered and subject to moments of depression and discouragement. However, Luther's human frailties could never undermine his unique place in history as the founder of and driving force behind the Reformation.

Which of the seven attributes of *Society's Secret Sauce - Eccentric People* - do you think Martin Luther most exemplified?

(1) Nonconforming Attitude
(2) Creative
(3) Intense Curiosity
(4) Idealistic
(5) Highly intelligent
(6) Opinionated
(7) Outspoken

Chapter 7

VINCENT van GOGH

"What would life be if we had no courage to attempt anything?"

Vincent van Gogh

Vincent Willem van Gogh, (Born March 30, 1853, Died July, 29, 1890) was a Dutch post-Impressionist painter whose influence in the world of art continues up to the present day. Some have gone so far as to state that he is the 'founder of modern art'. While his artistic talents were gargantuan, art critics are known to be pretentious and extremely subjective in their assessment of the quality of a painting. Nonetheless, regardless of whether or not Vincent van Gogh was the founder of modern art, the consensus is that his talent as an artist was enormous.

Born to middle class parents, van Gogh was a precocious child. He didn't paint until his late twenties but began drawing at a very young age. Since adulthood, finding galleries showing little interest in his art, he found his passion for art remained, leading him to work for firms of art dealers in various European countries, including England, France and Holland. In spite of his art being rejected by the critics, he completed over a thousand drawings, prints and sketches and nearly 900 oil paintings.

Vincent van Gogh displayed throughout his life creativity, a keen intellect, a definitive nonconformist streak, a strongly idealistic nature, and a deep curiosity about eclectic aspects of life. He was also opinionated and outspoken in his unrelenting efforts to have his art recognized. Vincent van Gogh never lost his idealistic belief that a loving spirit would one day, sooner or later, validate his belief in the value of his artistic creations. He remained perseverant throughout his lifetime in the face of constant rejection and the excoriation of his art by the critics. The fact that van Gogh did endure is a testament to his courage. Historical figures from an earlier era, who obviously cannot be interviewed today, are sometimes penetratingly revealed through their own statements. Here are a few telling excerpts of Vincent van Gogh in his own words:

I feel that there is nothing more truly artistic than to love people.

Love many things, for therein lies the true strength, and whosoever loves much performs much, and can accomplish much, and what is done in love is done well.

I wish they would only take me as I am.

The fishermen know that the sea is dangerous and the storm terrible, but they have never found these dangers sufficient reason for remaining ashore.

One must work and dare if one really wants to live.

Courage is often associated with the risk of physical harm, for example the bravery of soldiers risking their lives for a just cause on the field of battle. It is however equally courageous in a different way to stand bravely against the constant wounding of one's spirit. A proverb from the Old Testament of the King James translation of the Bible in 1603 states that *"The spirit of a man will sustain his infirmity, but a wounded spirit who can bear?"* Variations of this pithy bit of wisdom are found in the sacred texts of most of the world's religions. In modern English this proverb means that the spirit inside a man or woman beset by physical pain is more powerful than the physical pain they are presently enduring and will enable them to overcome that pain, but a spirit wounded by spiritual maladies such as sorrow, grief or depression is unbearable. The difficulty of bearing a spiritual as opposed to physical pain is attested to by the rate of suicides by people suffering from depression or grief. The spiritual pain that Vincent van Gogh endured for most of his adult life was so severe that his pain eventually became completely unbearable and resulted in his taking his own life.

He was very religious as a younger man and aspired to be a pastor, but not having any formal training, from 1879 -1880 he worked as a missionary in a mining section in Belgium where he also sketched people from the local community. His first notable work was 1885's *The Potato Eaters*. His palette at the time was mainly comprised of somber earth tones and showed no sign of the vivid coloration that distinguished his later and most famous paintings. His foray into religious work was however short lived because more dominant in his personality was an extremely independent mode of viewing life that was more consistent with free thinkers than the constraints of religion.

Exhibiting his nonconformist spirit, in 1880 he moved to Brussels, Belgium and resided in a part of the city where other free thinkers lived. During his stay there, friends described him as confrontational, prickly, and extremely opinionated. He lacked social skills because he often was caught up in imaginative ideas for his next painting. His lack of social skills stemmed from a mind that was preoccupied with art and from his creative, curious, highly intelligent, opinionated and outspoken personality. Vincent van Gogh was also very idealistic, believing ardently that his artwork was original and unique and could make an important contribution to the world of art.

In March 1886 he relocated to Paris and remained in France until his death. The French Impressionists of that era influenced his own paintings markedly. Later, he moved to the south of France and it is thought by many art experts that he was influenced by the region's bright and strong sunlight. During his sojourn in southern France his paintings grew much brighter in color, and he developed the unique and highly recognizable style that came to fruition during his stay in Arles, France in 1888. While many of his most famous oil paintings date to his time spent in southern France, in his lifetime these same paintings that are now regarded as masterpieces of art were scoffed at and disregarded. Sadly, Vincent van Gogh's works of art were never appreciated by others until after his death.

Some art critics have contended that van Gogh was near-sighted and that this was the reason many of his paintings lacked realism. However, van Gogh felt his critics lacked vision and were locked into a complacency that was not forward thinking when it came to styles of painting that were different than what was popular with the then prevailing mainstream views of the art world. His nonconformist and idealistic nature prevented him from changing his style of painting simply because Realism and the style of the French Impressionists and post-Impressionists were then the most accepted forms of art. A true eccentric, Vincent van Gogh would not be swayed by every passing trend in the art world.

Vincent van Gogh was like any artist also an emotional man who felt things deeply, and as a result he became tormented by the disparagement of his paintings by the art world because he knew that his paintings were creatively original and unique despite the mockery he received from art critics. This rejection of his artwork by art critics created a conundrum for van Gogh because he could not pierce the prosaic and pedestrian attitudes of his critics but neither could he forsake his own belief in the value of his artwork. An idealistic man of strong principles, he refused to change his unique style of painting to gain the approbation and approval of those who dismissed his artwork as nothing more than the odd manifestations of an insane mind. This increased van Gogh's frustration and caused him much sadness, pain, inner turmoil and anguish. Sadly, no one at the time ever considered that he was an innovative eccentric except Vincent van Gogh, who on several occasions expressed his belief that he was eccentric but not insane. Van Gogh did not do this to vainly draw attention to himself but to try to help his critics and detractors realize that he was not insane, as he was often accused of being.

After years of anxiety and frequent bouts of depression that were spawned by his inability to comprehend, rightfully so, the reasons why his contemporaries could neither see nor appreciate the value he saw in the type of artwork he created, his behavior became increasingly erratic. For example, he tried to engage in a razor fight with Paul Gauguin, the French post-Impressionist painter. He eventually became so distraught that he cut off a part of his own right ear with a knife; one of his most famous paintings is of his bandaged ear that he partially severed with a knife. Vincent van Gogh died at the age of 37 from a self inflicted gunshot wound that many believe was precipitated by the inner turmoil and pain he felt as a result of his reputation as a failed artist and a social outcast.

As is the case with all people, van Gogh was not without his faults. The fact that he committed suicide, even though he undoubtedly took such a drastic action because he could no longer cope with life, is not an excuse for a lack of fortitude that would have compelled him to instead forge onward in spite of his rejection by the art critics and the mockery he received from people who knew him personally. Vincent van Gogh was an artistic genius but it can also be argued that he should have worked more on improving his social skills and smoothing the rough edges of his countenance and demeanor, and that had he done so he might have received a more favorable response to his artwork.

The extent to which his mental health affected his painting has been widely debated. However, van Gogh's cutting off his right ear was an eccentric action that for him epitomized the anguish he felt as a result of his paintings and his other works of art being disregarded and unappreciated in his lifetime.

There has been some posthumous speculation that the reason he cut off his ear was because he suffered from Meniere's Disease, a disorder of the inner ear that is characterized by episodes of the sufferer of this disease visually seeing the world around him spinning round faster and faster, causing extreme vertigo and often resulting in the individual collapsing to the ground, unable to maintain sufficient balance to remain upright. Because there is no known cure for this disease and causal factors are also largely unknown, van Gogh would have experienced what for him and other sufferers of this inner ear disorder was unbearable agony. The point is that if the causal factor in van Gogh cutting off his right ear was in fact this disease or the result of the artistic anguish he felt at the rejection of his artwork, or a combination of both of these factors, his eccentricity was the fuel behind the radical action he took in cutting off his right ear, not insanity.

Think for a moment if the attitude of the majority of people in any field was that perfection had already been achieved. If that were the case, everything from art to science to music to concepts of government that contemplated something better, something filled with more truth, would hardly be received with open arms. The result would be utter stagnation and the end of progressive ideas for a better way of doing things. Vincent van Gogh was understandably frustrated by the art world's refusal to value his artwork primarily because his critics were content with the status quo.

Despite a widespread tendency today to romanticize his ill health, art historians of his time saw only an artist deeply frustrated by the inactivity and incoherence wrought through mental illness. Because the concept that van Gogh might merely be eccentric and not mentally ill was not contemplated by his friends and peers, the stigma of insanity that was foisted upon him played a significant part in the unhappiness that plagued him throughout his adult life, even though his late paintings show an artist at the height of his abilities, completely in control. According to art critic Robert Hughes, van Gogh's paintings were "longing for concision and grace", whatever that means.

Art critics can bloviate with the best of them, and any assessment of the life of Vincent van Gogh should never be left solely to the purview of fatuous art critics. I am reminded here of one of my many trips to Paris, France. I led a group of seven friends who had never been to France before on a tourist's view of the city that included the Louvre. After we toured the Louvre I wandered by myself a short distance ahead of the others and chanced upon a small building with about a dozen sculptures in it, most of them life sized, full bodied sculptures. One of the statues caught my attention because it was a sculpture of a woman that, unlike the others, rested upon a large square concrete pedestal with a few lines in French inscribed on the front side of the pedestal that this very beautiful work of art stood upon. Having taken French in college I walked up to the statue and read the inscription on the pedestal. Then, wanting to see the sculpture from all angles, I walked behind the statue and in so doing found myself walking through a puddle of dog piss!

Wanting to share this 'unique' experience with my seven friends, I went back to the group and told them that they should really see a very famous sculpture. So, we all went into the building that housed this particular sculpture and I had my seven friends stand in a horizontal line about twenty feet in front of the sculpture while I was halfway between them and the sculpture. I have a quirky sense of humor, so I began to expound and expatiate upon utter fabricated bullshit about this statue. As I was speaking, about twenty English speaking tourists came into the building, and seeing me in a three piece tailored suit expounding with authority on the significance of the statue, they assumed I was a tour guide so they eagerly joined what had then become a cue. I now had about thirty people in front of me, listening intently to what I was saying about this sculpture.

As I said, I have a rather offbeat and at times silly sense of humor that was fully engaged at that moment, but not devoid of a good motive. I told this group, now consisting of about thirty tourists, a ridiculous bogus story that the real value of the sculpture of this lady was to be found in an inscription in both French and English on the back side of the pedestal that many believed was a startling revelation concerning the authenticity of Michelangelo's paintings and sculptures. My 'tour group' readily bought into this complete bullshit I was spewing forth in a very authoritative manner. There was in fact no inscription on the back side of the pedestal. My goal, you see, was to get them to walk behind the statue and 'read' this nonexistent inscription so that they would all walk through the huge puddle of dog piss abutting the back side of the pedestal. They all lined up dutifully and one by one the tourist group, now lined up in a straight line, walked behind the sculpture and stepped into the 'aromatic' liquid tonic of dog urine. Since they had just been tricked, they appreciated the humor of the situation and wanted the rest of the members of the tour group to endure what they did, so they said nothing as they walked around the statue back to the front side of this sculpture.

I thought it was uproariously funny and so did about three quarters of these tourists, despite the fact that our shoes and socks and nylons had just been immersed in dog piss! I doubt that today any of these thirty people remember much if anything from the boring tour guides in the

Louvre, but to this day still remember that trip to Paris and the humorous fiasco they unwittingly took part in; I knew from my many travels abroad that it was funny little things like this that happened that made trips to foreign lands memorable. So what's the point of this story you might ask, and how is it relevant to Vincent van Gogh?

The point is that when it comes to works of art, beauty is best determined independently and not through the eyes of art experts or art critics no matter how authoritative they may seem. Had Vincent van Gogh been afforded this same courtesy of having his art evaluated independently and not through the prism of authoritative art experts or art critics, his life might not have ended at such a tragically young age. My 'tourist group' paid a price for blindly accepting the pronouncements of an authority figure, me - and I am by no means even remotely close to being any kind of an authority on art. Likewise, when we encounter a person who is unconventional and very opinionated in espousing their nonconformist beliefs that are radically different than what is considered 'normal', and are told by an authoritative figure that this quirky nonconformist person is insane, all too often we blindly accept their assertions as fact. In so doing we become as gullible as the tourists were that day in Paris who foolishly took the word of an "authority" figure as to the value of a sculpture and obeisantly walked behind the statue and into a puddle of dog piss.

The people who in Vincent van Gogh's lifetime saw nothing of value in his many paintings rejected van Gogh because they were people who followed the crowd and never considered that there might be something more to van Gogh's artistic creations. Vincent van Gogh did not deserve the misguided treatment of being told by a cadre of pompously foolish art critics that his paintings were worthless or the product of an insane mind. Likewise, eccentrics do not deserve to be mocked or disparaged or deemed insane simply because an authoritative figure adjudicates them to be worthy of only derision and denigration.

So, figuratively speaking, take a mental walk behind that statue in Paris and let your shoes be covered with dog piss; after all, a little dog piss never killed anyone. But we might learn or be reminded of an important truth, the one the tourists I fooled that day in Paris perceived: Just because an authority figure tells you a work of art is worthwhile, that doesn't make it so. Likewise, when someone tells you that eccentric people are insane, or denigrates them as fools and misfits, that doesn't make it so. Only a thorough investigation into the lives of people who appear to be odd or insane can enable us to determine whether any nonconformist individual is insane or is a true eccentric that is part of *'society's secret sauce', eccentricity*, and should therefore be greatly valued.

Vincent van Gogh received much opprobrium and scorn in his lifetime. His life was unlike other eccentric individuals such as Winston Churchill, John Lennon and Benjamin Franklin, who during their lifetimes were acknowledged for their exceptional contributions to society. Vincent van Gogh never experienced a good reception from the public for his paintings or approbation by the art world for his exceptional talent and abilities while he was alive.

In one of my recent trips abroad, this one to Amsterdam in The Netherlands, I visited the Vincent van Gogh museum in Amsterdam. Large crowds were there that day, and a deep, almost palpable appreciation for Vincent van Gogh's artistic ability was the overwhelmingly prevailing sentiment that I personally observed and felt. Vincent van Gogh was an eccentric artistic genius who created works of art that have for a very long time now been regarded posthumously as masterpieces of originality and creativity. But unfortunately the present day esteem for his paintings can do nothing to assuage, ameliorate or mollify the frustration, sadness, grief, torment and anguish that Vincent van Gogh experienced while he was alive.

In the popular BBC science fiction series *Doctor Who*, in an episode starring actor Matt Smith as 'The Doctor', the time traveling *Doctor Who* traveled back in time to meet Vincent van Gogh. He brought van Gogh into the 21st century where van Gogh observed the international acclaim that existed for his paintings and was comforted. Unfortunately, while the sadness of van Gogh's life was rectified in the world of science fiction, in his lifetime this was not the case.

Vincent van Gogh is an excellent example of what can happen when the eccentric genius of an individual is disregarded and unwelcome. For every success in history of eccentric people, there are likely ten other eccentrics like van Gogh who were not beloved by their peers in their lifetime. The frustration that van Gogh felt was summed up poignantly by John Lennon in looking back retrospectively on his own life:

> *"It was scary as a child, because there was nobody to relate to. Neither my auntie nor my friends nor anybody could ever see what I did. It was very, very scary and the only contact I had was reading about an Oscar Wilde or a Dylan Thomas or a van Gogh—all those books that my auntie had that talked about*

their suffering because of their visions. Because of what they saw, they were tortured by society for trying to express what they were. I saw loneliness."

Chapter 8

BENJAMIN FRANKLIN

"Search others for their virtues, thy self for thy vices."

Benjamin Franklin

B enjamin Franklin (Born January 6, 1705, Died April 17, 1790), possessed an abundance of all seven attributes of an eccentric person. His achievements in life were so voluminous and diverse that in this biographical synopsis of his life it is impossible to do more than recount only a portion of his many enduring accomplishments and the beneficial contributions to society he made during his lifetime. Aspects of Franklin's life that are either significant, singular, or are demarcation points for him could each constitute a separate book.

Benjamin Franklin was one of the Founding Fathers of the United States. Along with the other signatories to the Declaration of Independence he courageously risked his life by signing the Declaration of Independence because if the United States were defeated by the British in the Revolutionary War, Franklin and everyone else who signed this founding document risked execution by Great Britain. Sometimes the momentous occasion of the birth of the United States obscures the incredibly nonconformist spirt of not only Benjamin Franklin but of all the founding fathers; advocating for freedom from the rule of Great Britain at any cost was the ultimate act of defiance and nonconformity on the part of the patriots who freed the American colonies from the onerous rule of Great Britain.

A renowned scientist and a true creative genius filed with a curiosity that was an integral part of his entire life, Franklin was also a leading author, printer, political theorist and a politician. Franklin evinced early on in his career a proclivity towards the outspoken expression of his opinionated ideas. He was also a freemason, served as postmaster for the American colonies, and was an immensely creative and successful inventor. Franklin was also a civic activist, statesman, and diplomat. Benjamin Franklin was the epitome of a *Renaissance Man*.

As a scientist, he was a major figure in the American Enlightenment and the history of physics for his discoveries and theories regarding electricity. As an inventor, Franklin was prodigious. His most notable inventions include the lightning rod, a glass harmonica, bifocal glasses, and the Franklin stove. He was an integral force behind many civic organizations, including Philadelphia's fire department and a university. Franklin had such an intense and eclectic curiosity that he even studied ocean currents and demography.

Franklin was accorded the title of "The First American", even though for a period of about ten years from 1765 to 1775 when he lived in London, England as the representative for the American colonies to England, he still acknowledged the authority of King George III over the American colonies. Returning to America in 1775, his loyalty to the American Revolution and to the fledgling United States of America was steadfast and unwavering. During his decade in London, England, while Franklin accepted the authority of King George III over the British colonies in America, he was by no means a loyalist in support of the British Crown. Franklin sagaciously realized that he could not procure any benefits for the American colonies if he had not acquiesced to the authority of the British Crown. He masterfully kept his own inner longings for freedom and independence from Britain for the American colonies a surreptitious secret because he knew that he could be a much more effective advocate for the American colonists if he kept his true feelings to himself during his sojourn in England. He spent most of his time in London ardently advocating for the rights of the American colonies. For example, Franklin successfully pleaded the colonist's case for the repeal of the onerous and undemocratic stamp tax that the British imposed on the colonies.

He campaigned indefatigably for unity amongst the American colonies in their struggle for independence. From 1776 to 1785 Franklin served as the first ambassador to France, and when he returned to the United States in 1785 the only person who had more power than Franklin was George Washington. Franklin exemplified the nascent American spirit as well as the interests of the newly formed United States of America. He played a prominent role in defining the incipient American ideology as a combination of the practical values of hard work, education, community spirit and thrift. Franklin also promoted the importance of self-governing institutions.

Franklin had such a prodigious intellect that he could simultaneously apply himself to multiple unrelated matters. For example, he worked tirelessly to ensure the preservation and growth of the newly formed United States of America and at the same time promoted his opposition to authoritarianism in government, politics and religion while continuing unabated his study of electricity. Franklin's intensely curious mind never stopped applying itself to such a diverse and eclectic range of subjects that his friends often marveled not only at his achievements but also at his stamina.

Benjamin Franklin was a highly intelligent and idealistic individual capable of understanding that he should not allow his personal predilections to get in the way of pursuing any matter that he felt would benefit the newly formed nation. For example, even though he opposed religious authoritarianism he published the somewhat dogmatic writings and sermons of the famed evangelist George Whitefield, who played a pivotal role in creating the religious revival that spread throughout Great Britain and the United States known as the 'Great Awakening'.

George Whitefield and Benjamin Franklin became such good friends that Whitefield felt the liberty to engage Franklin in numerous discussions that endeavored to save Franklin's soul and convert him to Christianity, as it was well known that Franklin was not a particularly religious man. Despite Franklin's lack of evangelical fervor he decided to publish the sermons of the British evangelist George Whitefield because he believed that religion was a positive force in the nation because it assisted in the creation and maintenance of good values and a strong moral compass, something he felt was vital to the growth of the newly formed United States of America.

The genesis of Franklin's antiestablishment views came from a radical shift in thinking in Europe about the proper role of government and religion that generally speaking emphasized a logical and humanist perspective. Beliefs regarding scientific exploration and experimentation also changed. This change in the way that Europeans viewed the world began around 1715 and lasted until 1789 and was known as 'The Enlightenment'. The values of the Enlightenment then blooming in Europe found a keen ally in Franklin. He especially related to principles of the Enlightenment that stressed the value of the scientific method and that called for a total rejection of authoritarianism in government, politics and religion. The umbrella of tolerance that permeated pervasively through the Enlightenment was a principle that manifested itself in multiple ways that were beneficial to the progress of the newly formed United States.

According to historian Henry Steele Commager, *"In a Franklin could be merged the virtues of Puritanism without its defects, the illumination of the Enlightenment without its heat."* For another one of his biographers, Walter Isaacson, Franklin was *"the most accomplished American of his age and the most influential in inventing the type of society America would become."* Franklin's beneficial contributions to American society have had positive ramifications that have endured to this day.

Franklin became a successful newspaper editor and printer in Philadelphia, the leading city in the colonies. With two partners he published the *Pennsylvania Chronicle,* a newspaper that was known for its revolutionary sentiments and predilections and for criticisms of British policies. He became quite wealthy through publishing, especially with two publications, *Poor Richard's Almanack* and *The Pennsylvania Gazette.* Politically, Franklin was not only a signatory but a forceful contributor to the founding documents of the United States, the Declaration of Independence and the United States Constitution. Thomas Jefferson, later to become President Jefferson, wrote the Declaration of Independence with input from Benjamin Franklin. Franklin was the only Founding Father who was a signatory of four documents critical to the founding and survival of the newly formed United States - the Declaration of Independence, the United States Constitution, the Treaty of Alliance with France, and the Treaty of Paris.

He played a major role in establishing the University of Pennsylvania and was elected the first president of the American Philosophical Society. Franklin first became a national hero in America when as agent for the American colonies he spearheaded the successful effort to have Parliament in London repeal the unpopular Stamp Act. Franklin's gregariousness and loquaciousness combined with his brilliant mind, nonconformist beliefs, and opinionated, outspoken tongue lent themselves nicely to his many successes as a diplomat. He was widely admired among the French as the United States ambassador to France, living in Paris from 1776 until 1785. He was the major and decisively dispositive figure in the development of positive Franco-American relations. His efforts to gain support from the French for the American Revolution were a singular success of Franklin's because Franklin essentially unilaterally persuaded the French to send to the American colonies vast shipments of munitions that proved crucial to the eventual success and preservation of the American victory in their war against Great Britain for independence.

Benjamin Franklin had an incredibly impressive resume filled with consequential achievements whose effects have reverberated through the centuries. If you have found the life of Benjamin Franklin interesting it is because history isn't really a boring subject as some people think. So, with probably perfunctory apologies for the length of this review of Franklin's life, think of it as an opportunity to retake that history class you never cared for or undertake for the first time the exploration of historical events and realize thereby their judicious and beneficial application to your own life. Henry Ford said "History is bunk." The pioneering car maker was a master at creating and rolling off an assembly line gasoline powered automobiles and was adroit at making money, but I wouldn't take his advice on anything outside of the automotive or financial worlds. There is timeless truth in the old saying that *'Those who refuse to study history are destined to repeat its mistakes.'* History is actually quite useful and fascinating!

I will end my pitch for the value of history here. Turning our attention back to Benjamin Franklin, his service for many years as the British postmaster for the colonies enabled him to set up the first national communications network. This national communications network played a pivotal role in keeping the 13 colonies connected to each other politically and ideologically. He was also active in community affairs, colonial and state politics, as well as national and international affairs. From 1785 to 1788 he served as governor of Pennsylvania.

Originally a slaveowner, in 1762 he had an epiphany about the immorality and injustice of slavery and became a staunch believer in the principle that all men, regardless of skin color, were created equal under God. He freed all his slaves by 1770, an act that placed Franklin in the vanguard of the abolitionist movement and exemplified Franklin's non-conformist beliefs, intellectual acumen, outspoken courage, and idealistic nature. In Franklin's lifetime the white United States populace believed that slavery was legally, morally, and socially acceptable and not an egregious injustice to the many African Americans living in the United States. Franklin's compassion and forward thinking mind are illustrated by the fact that Great Britain did not abolish slavery until 1833 and the United States did not follow suit until the 1860s during the Civil War at the behest of President Abraham Lincoln. Franklin's unique ability to crystallize the most important issues at hand combined with his belief in equality and justice for all enabled Franklin to become one of the first leaders of his era to adopt an enlightened abolitionist attitude concerning slavery.

The life of Benjamin Franklin reveals a man accomplished in many diverse fields, such as scientific inventions, demography, electricity, printing, philosophical theories concerning virtue and religion, and most notably political achievements for which he achieved his status as one of America's most influential Founding Fathers. The totality of his achievements in life are almost mind numbing. Franklin has been honored on U.S. coins and is still the face of the $100 bill. Additionally, everything from warships to educational institutions to cities to corporations bear his name and are a testament to his lasting influence upon the United States of America.

Benjamin Franklin was also very opinionated and outspoken about his rejection of all religious dogma, including Christianity. At the same time his idealistic nature compelled him to show great tolerance and respect for all churches; he even advocated for the rights of churches. Though he was not religious, throughout his lifetime Franklin maintained the values of the Puritans, values that included his devotion to education, egalitarianism, thrift, industry, honesty, charity, temperance, and the promotion of a community spirit. Franklin displayed his idealistic nature and impassioned intellect by not allowing his own personal beliefs about God and religion to interfere with his belief that religion and churches had a vital and necessary part to play in forging the evolving spirit of the newly formed United States. In fact, he believed that the United States would survive only if the people were virtuous, and religion played an essential role in helping people live a virtuous life. Despite Franklin's support for religion and churches, his personal rejection of Christianity and all religions was a very nonconformist position to take considering the fact that the fledgling United States was during his lifetime overwhelmingly a Christian nation.

Benjamin Franklin was however, like every other person who ever lived, imperfect and flawed. His marriage was a common law marriage, he fathered an illegitimate son, and he often exhibited traits of a blatant social climber both during his sojourns in Great Britain and in France.

Eccentricity was also a central part of Franklin's nature; his nonconformist spirit and idealistic nature reverberated through almost everything he did in his life. For example, at a dinner in France with members of the French nobility and the renowned chemist Joseph Priestly, a very opinionated Benjamin Franklin opined to Priestly that it would be a notable achievement on Priestly's part if he could invent a spray that would immediately neutralize the odor of "farts". The members of the French aristocracy present at that dinner were not a little taken aback and nonplussed by Franklin's 'undignified' suggestion to Priestly. Never one to back down from his beliefs, Franklin even went so far as to attempt to prove that European intellectuals were far too pretentious and concerned about unimportant matters when it came to science by writing an essay entitled *'Fart Proudly'* to show the importance he believed researching bodily matters should have.

Franklin also practiced 'air bathing', for better health. At the time, the common wisdom was that cold weather caused sickness. Ben, however, believed that people were the problem and being cooped up all winter with each other led to sickness, so he would sit in the wintertime at an open window, stark naked, to help with air circulation and disease prevention. While an innovative idea, this was also eccentric behavior.

Another example of Franklin's eccentricity is that he practiced what was then a new approach to debating public issues of significance by what we now call "sock puppetry", which uses multiple aliases of authorship to give the appearance that many people had similar views, and sometimes Franklin argued opposing views. Franklin's most famous alter ego when engaging in this tactic was Silence Dogood.

While 'sock puppetry' is not an uncommon journalistic approach today, in Franklin's day it was both uncommon and nonconformist. Eccentric acts or beliefs frequently later become an accepted part of mainstream culture even though at the time of their expression they were deemed nonconformist.

To illustrate the preceding point, in the days of the English kings in medieval England, their rule was by the ubiquitous belief in 'divine right'; the concept of 'divine right' held that the kings of England were appointed by divine decree of God. If the medieval kings had been able to glimpse into life in England several centuries later, they would have been shocked and appalled to learn that England was now ruled by the mainstream, present day accepted belief that its citizens be governed by a democratically elected House of Commons and headed by a democratically elected prime minister, with the monarchy retaining only a titular and ceremonial role devoid of any real governing authority.

Resuming our examination of some of Benjamin Franklin's eccentric acts, on one occasion Franklin exhibited his eccentric nature by nearly electrocuting himself trying to kill and cook a turkey with electricity. After Franklin's death in 1790, a large number of bodies were found in the basement of Franklin' house. It was presumed that they were taken by

Franklin from graveyards to study human anatomy, which was in its infancy in those days. At the time not only was Franklin's exhumation of the dead against the law, it exemplified Franklin's eccentric nature and his willingness to reach beyond the often stagnant status quo.

Many other examples of Franklin's eccentricity throughout his lifetime exist, but unfortunately, in order to ensure that this book is not inordinately lengthy they are left to the reader to discover if so inclined. However, one additional example worth noting is that on one occasion Franklin nearly lost his life chasing a "wind-spout", or tornado, in Maryland to help prove his theory that water spouts were really made of air. While this was arguably a foolhardy thing to do, it also displayed what a courageous individual Benjamin Franklin was.

The record of the life of Benjamin Franklin reveals a true *Renaissance Man*, a brilliant thinker with a great mind, an astute politician and diplomat, an innovative and extremely creative scientist, a prescient leader, and so much more. However, if Franklin had not possessed an eccentric spirit his many accomplishments and beneficial contributions to society might never have occurred at all or been very severely circumscribed. The record of Benjamin Franklin's life indicates a man who possessed an abundance of all seven attributes of an eccentric person:

(1) Nonconforming Attitude

(2) Creative

(3) Intense Curiosity

(4) Idealistic

(5) Highly intelligent

(6) Opinionated

(7) Outspoken

Which of these seven attributes of eccentric people in your estimation typified the life of Benjamin Franklin *in the most notable manner?*

Chapter 9

LORD BYRON

"Be thou the rainbow in the storms of life. The evening beam that smiles the clouds away, and tints tomorrow with prophetic ray."

Lord Byron

George Gordon Byron, the 6th Baron Byron, (Born January 22, 1788, died April 19, 1824), commonly known simply as Lord Byron, was an English poet, a leading figure in the Romantic movement in literature, and one of England's well known 19th century eccentrics. Lord Byron's first major success as a poet was his narrative poem *Childe Harold's Pilgrimage*, a lengthy four part narrative poem. Large portions of this poem are believed to be autobiographical. Byron is also well known for *Don* Juan, another of his lengthy narrative poems, and the short lyric poem *She Walks in Beauty*. Byron also wrote many other works of poetry.

Byron is regarded as one of the greatest British poets, especially by himself, considering Shakespeare to be a hack as a writer. Of Shakespeare Lord Byron said: "*Shakespeare's name, you may depend on it, stands absurdly too high and will go down.*" Lord Byron remains widely read and influential. He travelled extensively across Europe, especially in Italy where he lived for seven years. Later in life, Byron displayed great courage of his convictions when he joined the Greek War of Independence against the Ottoman Empire.

He did not live long enough to die in battle, succumbing instead to ill health, but he was able to help the Greek quest for independence with large sums of money and armaments, and it was fully his intention to enter the battlefields as a soldier alongside the Greeks. For his love of Greece many Greeks revere him unto the present day as a national hero. He died about a year after arriving in Greece from a fever he contracted in Missolonghi, which was then held by Greece and is today part of modern Greece. Byron died at the young age of 36. Courage was a hallmark of his brief life.

Often described as the most flamboyant and notorious of the major Romantics, Byron was both celebrated and castigated in life for his aristocratic excesses, including accumulating huge debts and having numerous love affairs with men as well as women. Byron, who was very opinionated and outspoken, had no compunctions about carrying on a sexual relation with his own half sister, which by any standard is nonconformist and unconventional. Byron also engaged in self imposed periods of exile. He would oftentimes confine his diet to consuming only biscuits and wine or strange vegetarian meals that he created. Lord Byron was in his day the ultimate nonconformist. He was outspoken about what he believed was truth, was extremely intelligent, idealistic, quite opinionated, and a highly creative individual. Byron also possessed at least two of the four secondary attributes of an eccentric person inasmuch as he was sometimes not interested in the opinions or company of other people and had a mischievous sense of humor.

Lord Byron fathered several children but only one child, Augusta Ada King-Noel, a famous mathematician, was a legitimate offspring of Lord Byron. All of Byron's other children were born out of wedlock. In an era long before proof of parentage could be proved by DNA comparison and when rumors were rife and were often regarded as synonymous with truth, he was accused of and disparaged for fathering children out of wedlock. Lord Byron's sexual escapades and his eccentricities were by no means looked upon favorably by his early 19th century contemporaries, but Byron didn't really care what his critics thought about his sexual life or the flamboyance that was a part of his nature because a genuine spirit of nonconformism burned brightly in his life.

Byron's flamboyance and cavalier attitudes resulted in Byron lacking moderation in the conduct of his life and this was perhaps his greatest flaw next to his personal hubris and arrogant attitudes towards other people. As a child Byron was spoiled by his mother who never had much success in inculcating moralistic values that were in tune with contemporary society. As a result Byron never really cared that the public often disparaged him for accumulating excessive debts and for carrying on homosexual affairs with a number of different men. In spite of these character defects it must be understood that Lord Byron inherited large sums of money and became a titled aristocrat upon the death of his great uncle, the 5th Lord Byron, when Byron was only 10 years old. Inheriting huge sums of money and becoming a member of the English nobility at such a young age made Byron easily susceptible to the pitfalls of excessive immoderation in all aspects of his life.

It has been argued that Lord Byron lacked a truly idealistic nature because of his arrogance and because of his seeming willingness to use other people for his own personal gain, satisfaction or desires. However, if Byron had done nothing else in his life to make beneficial contributions to society other than inspiring the world to reach for the summit of lofty goals through his poetry and losing his life in Greece as a result of his courageous service to the Greeks in helping them in their noble cause of throwing off the oppressive yoke of the Ottoman Empire, his place in history as an idealistic soul would be assured. Sometimes poets can best be understood by the poetry they write because it emanates from the deepest recesses of the poet's heart. Here are a few examples of Byron's poetry reflective of his idealistic beliefs:

"Love will find a way through paths where wolves fear to prey."

"They never fail who die in a great cause."

"Adversity is the first path to truth."

"The beginning of atonement is the sense of its necessity."

"Those who will not reason, are bigots, those who cannot, are fools, and those who dare not, are slaves."

"Be thou the rainbow in the storms of life. The evening beam that smiles the clouds away, and tints tomorrow with prophetic ray."

"Men think highly of those who rise rapidly in the world; whereas nothing rises quicker than dust, straw, and feathers."

"Opinions are made to be changed - or how is truth to be got at?"

"The heart will break, but broken live on."

"There are four questions of value in life, Don Octavio. What is sacred? Of what is the spirit made? What is worth living for and what is worth dying for? The answer to each is the same. Only love."

For those who are unfamiliar with the poet Lord Byron, many scholars consider him to be the second best English poet after Shakespeare, though as previously mentioned Byron would beg to differ, as Byron was also an arrogant and impetuous man who did not hesitate to proclaim his own greatness as a poet. His peers often begged to differ however with what they believed was Byron's inflated opinion of himself, which historians have speculated was his method of compensating for feelings of inferiority because he was lame in one foot.

A contemporary of his, Lord Holland, at a gathering of Lord Holland's, praised Byron fulsomely in Lord Byron's presence and in the company of other guests also present at Lord Holland's gathering in his home. But in Lord Holland's memoirs written well after this social event, Holland said that while the poet's speech was full of fancy, wit, and invective, Lord Byron was not well reasoned and neither was his personality well balanced. Lord Holland was not alone amongst Byron's critics who judged him harshly, however notwithstanding his detractors his legacy remains as one of England's greatest poets. Byron also influenced many poets who came after him.

Lord Byron also possessed the thread that binds eccentrics, courage, and in no small measure. In spite of his lameness in one foot, he took fencing lessons from Henry Angelo and boxing lessons from John 'Gentleman' Jackson, a famous boxing champion. Byron was doggedly determined, as was his personal hero the hunchback Alexander Pope, that his lameness would neither blight nor curtail his prowess.

His eccentricity was first seen when as a student at Cambridge University's Trinity College he wanted to keep a dog in his room. When Cambridge's authorities informed him that university regulations did not allow him to keep a dog, he was so annoyed by what he judged to be a draconian rule that he searched for and found a loophole in university rules about keeping animals on campus; bears were not specifically prohibited as were dogs. In *History Revealed,* in an article about Lord Byron from their November 10th, 2014 issue, the magazine reported as follows regarding Lord Byron and his tame bear cub:

"Lord Byron argued that as bears weren't specifically mentioned in their statutes the college had no legal grounds for complaint. Where he acquired the animal isn't clear but it may have been from a traveling menagerie. Byron won the argument against the college and the bear stayed with him in his lodgings. He would walk the bear around the grounds of Trinity on a chain like a dog, and delighted in the reactions he got from passersby.

"Not finished yet, however, Byron even suggested that he would apply for the bear to join the college. He once wrote:

"I have got a new friend, the finest in the world, a tame bear. When I brought him here, they asked me what I meant to do with him, and my reply was, 'he should sit for a fellowship'."

Lord Byron's nonconformist spirit, his creativity, intense curiosity, idealism, great intelligence, and his opinionated and outspoken nature were evident throughout his life. For example, towards the end of his life his eccentricity remained on full display when during a journey from Genoa, Italy to Pisa, Italy he traveled in an ostentatious coach, not only with all his furnishings but with a menagerie of animals which included three pet geese hanging in cages from the back of his coach. Lord Byron suffered much personal pain and anguish during his lifetime because the concept that he was eccentric was never considered as the force behind his odd and socially unacceptable behavior.

This biographical synopsis of Lord Byron and those of all twelve eccentric people examined in this book are just that - synopses that are by no means meant to serve as complete biographies of any of these individuals but that which is sufficient to illustrate their eccentricity and the positive impact eccentricity had on their respective accomplishments and contributions to society in their diverse fields of expertise. With respect to Lord Byron the beneficial contributions he made to poetry remain indisputable and his opinionated, outspoken and nonconformist nature was evident throughout his personal life. His poetry exemplified not only his creativity but his curious nature and his intellectual acumen, and the totality of his brief life reveals a man possessed of all seven attributes of eccentric people:

(1) Nonconforming attitude

(2) Creative

(3) Intense curiosity

(4) Idealistic

(5) Highly intelligent

(6) Opinionated

(7) Outspoken

Eccentricity in individuals did not stop with Lord Byron but continues to be an essential component of the progression of society in the post World War II era and into the 21st century. The limitations of the length of this book circumscribe the ability to mention countless other eccentric souls like the renowned mathematics genius of ancient Greece, *Pythagoras,* the writer *Oscar Wilde* and the entrepreneurial technology innovator *Steve Jobs* to name but a few. These individuals have also contributed significantly to the advancement of society and culture, but the twelve people examined in this book, including Lord Byron, represent a sufficiently circumspect approach to eccentricity because of their diversity.

Furthermore, it is an unfortunate fact that the study of history is no longer held in the high esteem it was in previous generations, so, I have tried to limit the number of lives of eccentric individuals dealt with in this book in an attempt to strike a balance between sufficiently persuasive proof and a recognition that history is no longer one of the top three subjects of conversation in today's world!

The individuals whose lives are recounted herein are drawn from a time period spanning six centuries, with eight of them being from the 20th century. Their many contributions to western civilization were made from a diverse array of fields, including but not limited to: theology, poetry, art, government, astronomy, physics, electricity, writing, social movements, national independence movements, television, movies, political and economic thinking, and music. They provide a credible basis for the thesis of this book, i.e., *the value of being eccentric, and its concomitant corollary, the past, present and future value of eccentric people.*

Chapter 10

HISTORICAL ECCENTRICITY: 20th CENTURY

"A free society cherishes nonconformity. It knows from the non-conformist, from the eccentric, have come many of the great ideas."

Henry Steele Commager

As stated previously, though deemed unconventional, peculiar and even radical in their extant milieu, the engines of profound positive changes in society have often been eccentrics. History is replete with examples illustrating that forward movement in society is led by those considered - in the time of the advent of the exposition of their new ideas - radical and eccentric for their time. This section will introduce eight people who are considered to have made enormous contributions to society yet were also eccentric:

(1) Albert Einstein

(2) Nikola Tesla

(3) Winston Churchill

(4) Pablo Picasso

(5) Mahatma Gandhi

(6) Raymond Burr

(7) Ayn Rand

(8) John Lennon

As you are about to read biographical facts about the lives of these eight people, a salient thing to bear in mind is the existence of their eccentricity, reflected by each possessing in common all seven attributes of eccentric people:

(1) Nonconforming Attitude

(2) Creative

(3) Intense Curiosity

(4) Idealistic

(5) Highly intelligent

(6) Opinionated

(7) Outspoken

Everyone conforms to various social, economic and other norms and this is a good thing. But few would argue that conformity should be the overriding aspect of a person's character and personality. If we took the position that conforming trumps other personality attributes one could possess, then it would be difficult to deem the personality attributes eccentric people have in common, such as the qualities of creativity, idealism, and a high degree of curiosity about life, of much value.

As the lives of these eight accomplished individuals are about to be discussed, in all likelihood the first thing that would _not_ come to mind is their eccentric nature! But as you read on I think you will find that eccentricity was an inextricable part of their natures and a major causal factor that fueled their respective achievements.

Chapter 11

ALBERT EINSTEIN

"Few people are capable of expressing with equanimity opinions which differ from the prejudices of their social environment. Most people are incapable of forming such opinions."

Albert Einstein

Albert Einstein, (Born March 14, 1879, Died April 18, 1955) was a German born theoretical physicist with a maverick streak ingrained in his nature. Einstein was an indisputably brilliant man who was gifted with an amazing level of intelligence. He also had a boundless curiosity and an original mind filled with creative approaches to various conundrums he encountered in the field of physics. The above quotation of Einstein reflects an opinionated and outspoken spirit that was an integral part of his nature throughout his life. He developed the general theory of relativity, one of the two pillars of modern physics (alongside quantum mechanics). Einstein's work is also known for its influence on the philosophy of science. Einstein is best known in popular culture for his mass–energy equivalence formula $E = mc^2$, which is widely regarded as 'the world's most famous equation'. He received the 1921 Nobel Prize in Physics for his 'services to theoretical physics', in particular for his discovery of the law of the photoelectric effect, a pivotal and vital step in the evolution of quantum theory.

Long before he became famous, Einstein remained steadfast in his ability and willingness to be a serenely amused loner who was quite comfortable being very nonconformist in every aspect of his life. Independent in his thinking from a young age, his imagination enabled him to break from the often suffocating and stifling confines of conventional wisdom. Einstein's probing mind operated at its own unique pace and at its own timetable, reminiscent of what Peruvians call *'Peruvian time'.*

During one of my trips to Lima, Peru, my business included meeting someone at my hotel in Lima at 2:00 p.m. The time of the meeting was set the previous day and reconfirmed the morning of the meeting. A couple of minutes before 2:00 p.m. I pulled out a chair at the conference table in the hotel and sat down and waited for the arrival of the individual I was scheduled to meet with. 2:00 p.m. and then 2:25 p.m. came and went and I was still alone at the conference table. I checked my watch again at 2:40 p.m. local time but I was still the only person in the conference room of my hotel.

Finally at 10 minutes to 3:00 p.m. my Peruvian counterpart appeared. Waiting for someone to arrive at a pre-set time for almost an hour before the person shows up is considered by most western businesspeople as extremely rude. When I very kindly confronted him with the fact that he was almost a full hour late for our meeting, he gently laughed and said, *"Oh, you are operating on American time. Here in Peru we operate on Peruvian time."* Inquiring of him what *'Peruvian time'* was, he explained to me that in Peru if a meeting was scheduled for 2:00 p.m. one could expect the parties to that meeting to show up anytime between 2:00 p.m. and 3:00 p.m. and that such tardiness would never be deemed a breach of the rules of business or social decorum. Thus, Einstein, who could not stand to be suffocated by the confines or constrictions of conventional wisdom, governed his life in a laid back fashion similar to *'Peruvian time'*. Just as the Peruvians have their own unique way of measuring time, Einstein had his own unique way of evaluating not only time but the universe and everything in it.

Einstein's nonconformist attitude was not only evident throughout his lifetime in his personality but in his political views as well. Although he valued socialist ideology, he was too much of an individualist to be comfortable with excessive state control or centralized authority.

Einstein is on record as saying *"Imagination is more important than knowledge."* This belief inevitably led him to embrace nonconformity. To the lover and woman who would one day become his wife he said this: *"Long live impudence! It is my guardian angel in this world."* Many have argued that in fact Einstein's success in life was the result of his challenging authority, questioning conventional wisdom, and marveling with a wondrous amazement at mysteries that others deemed merely mundane. Throughout his lifetime Albert Einstein retained the awe and curiosity of a child, never losing his sense of wonder at what he regarded as nature's magical phenomena such as gravity, inertia, acceleration, magnetic fields and light beams. He wrote to a friend later in life that *"People like you and me never grow old. We never cease to stand like curious children before the great mystery into which we were born."* Such beliefs are at the heart of the very essence of eccentric minds.

Skepticism, including that of religion and accepted wisdom became a trademark of his approach to life. In a 1901 letter to a friend he said *"A foolish faith in authority is the worst enemy of truth."* Ganesh Hoffmann, a colleague and collaborator of Einstein's later in Einstein's life summed up well Einstein's eccentric nature when he wrote of Einstein that *"His early suspicion of authority, which never wholly left him, was to prove of decisive importance. Without it he would not have been able to develop the powerful independence of mind that gave him the courage to challenge established scientific beliefs and thereby revolutionize physics."* Mr. Hoffmann's description of Einstein's unconventional, nonconformist spirit stands as a succinct but eloquent affirmation of one of the most important personality attributes of eccentric people.

Near the beginning of his career, Einstein thought that then widely accepted principles of Newtonian theories were no longer enough to reconcile the laws of classical mechanics with the laws of the electromagnetic field. This led to the development of his special theory of relativity. He also realized that the principle of relativity could be extended to gravitational fields.

In 2016 Einstein's theories on gravitational fields were proven true by leading physicists, which theorem postulated that the time line of the universe was bent and not linear. This 2016 discovery based upon Einstein's original theory opens the theoretical door of the possibility of travel back in time.

Along with his theory of gravitation, in 1916 he published a paper on general relativity. He continued to deal with problems of statistical mechanics and quantum theory, which led to his explanations of particle theory and the motion of molecules. He also investigated the thermal properties of light that laid the foundation of the photon theory of light.

In 1917, Einstein applied the general theory of relativity to model the large scale structure of the universe. He was visiting the United States when Adolf Hitler came to power in 1933 and, being Jewish, did not go back to Germany because of its growing persecution of Jews and the establishment of an authoritarian regime. He had been a professor at the Berlin Academy of Sciences. He settled in the U.S., becoming an American citizen in 1940.

On the eve of World War II, he endorsed a letter to President Roosevelt alerting him to the potential development by Nazi Germany of "extremely powerful bombs of a new type" and recommending that the U.S.

begin similar research, thereby revealing his idealistic belief in the value of preserving democratic institutions. Einstein's intellectual prowess and genius still dominate perceptions of him, but he was also a deeply idealistic man who genuinely wanted to make the world a better place for other people.

Einstein's letter to President Roosevelt eventually led to what would become the Manhattan Project, the successful attempt by the United States government to create an atomic bomb. Einstein supported defending the Allied forces, but his idealistic nature led him to denounce the idea of using the newly discovered nuclear fission as a weapon. Later, with the famous British philosopher Bertrand Russell, Einstein signed the Russell–Einstein Manifesto, which highlighted the danger of nuclear weapons. Albert Einstein was affiliated with the Institute for Advanced Study in Princeton, New Jersey, until his death in 1955.

Einstein published more than 300 scientific papers along with over 150 non-scientific works. On December 5, 2014, universities and archives announced the release of Einstein's papers, comprising more than 30,000 unique documents. His intellectual achievements and originality have made the word "Einstein" synonymous with "genius".

Conversely Albert Einstein wasn't a genius who was so precocious that he manifested signs of his brilliant mind from a very early age. Instead he struggled to use language as a child, causing his parents and his physicians great concern and even consternation. Einstein did eventually become skilled in the use of language and from his teenage years onward utilized his newfound linguistic skills to express his stubborn, precocious, nonconformist and outspoken rejection of authority. Musing upon his slowed early development as a child, Einstein said that this gave him greater opportunities to think about life's basic elements, like space and time. His sense of wonder at these concepts made him pose curious questions, eventually leading to such breakthroughs as his theory of relativity. Fortunately for the advancement of science, Einstein never grew out of either the sense of awe and amazement with which he viewed the universe or his willingness to buck the status quo.

Albert Einstein was a complex person. As a young man he was aware of his mental prowess but spent years in a middle level boring bureaucratic job in Germany's patent office. His rise to top positions in the field of physics and his later revolutionary discoveries and breakthroughs in physics did not follow a meteoric trajectory. In fact there was a period in Einstein's adult life wherein his peers could see no potential for greatness in Einstein, which understandably led to his feelings of frustration. Frustration can have a negative or a positive effect on a person. The negative effect manifests itself by causing us to give up our dreams and in so doing eliminate frustration from our lives at the steep price of forsaking our dreams and goals. For Einstein, the frustration he felt had a positive effect on him because it spurred him onward with renewed fervor to become all that he knew he could become. In that process of transforming himself from a clerk in the patent office filing patents into a brilliant physicist he embraced his eccentric nature.

For example, his chauffeur reported that he once plucked a grasshopper off the ground and ate it. He would also take his violin along on birdwatching treks, playing music with tears streaming down his face. And, in spite of arriving at a stage in life where he was relatively financially prosperous enough to easily afford purchasing his own cigarettes, Einstein would pick up off the streets and sidewalks filthy half smoked cigarettes butts, light them, and smoke them instead of buying his own new pack of cigarettes.

An insight into the eccentric life of Albert Einstein has been provided in a November 6, 2005 issue of the British newspaper *The Daily Telegraph,* commonly referred to as simply *The Telegraph*. *The Telegraph*, in production since 1858, is well regarded as a 'newspaper of record' that is sold throughout the United Kingdom and internationally. It has an excellent reputation for high quality, with the BBC describing it as 'one of the world's great titles'. *The Telegraph* reported that: 'In a letter written by Albert Einstein to his favorite grandson, Bernhard Caesar Einstein, 75, who has never previously spoken about his famous relative, Bernhard recounted a string of anecdotes about the often bizarre life of the 20th century's greatest scientist.'

"At one point, the younger Mr. Einstein recalled, his grandfather resorted to collecting cigarette butts from the streets to circumvent his doctor's effort to stop him from smoking. In this letter, filed away and forgotten for seven years, Albert Einstein's grandson also recalled receiving a baffling three hour lecture from Einstein on the mathematical properties of soap bubbles. He was aged eight at the time. The lecture was delivered while the two were alone on a becalmed sailing boat. Einstein, his grandson recalled, deliberately went out sailing when there was no wind because he felt it was more challenging." Think for a moment if someone in the field of physics or with economic or employment control over Einstein observed what appeared to be a man with unkempt and unusual hair from a distance great enough so as not to personally recognize this man, but still close enough to see him bend over, pick up a half smoked cigarette from the street or sidewalk, pull out some matches and light the cigarette and begin to smoke it.

Supposing further in this hypothetical example, and in an age when eccentricity was not infrequently considered synonymous with insanity, that this same man with some sort of influence over Einstein's future continued walking in the direction of this odd man putting filthy, potentially germ infested cigarette butts from the street into his mouth and lighting and smoking them, and then quickened his pace and walked fast enough to catch up with him and recognized that this eccentric man was indeed Albert Einstein.

Remember, in this not too improbable hypothetical, it is unlikely that this individual with economic or employment or academic control over Einstein would have considered Einstein's behavior favorably. In fact, any prior respect for his work in the area of physics might have been diminished and Albert Einstein, because of his eccentricity, might have been relegated to the dustbins of history as a crazy person at worst or mentally unstable at best.

The preceding hypothetical scenario based upon the facts of Einstein's odd habit of smoking cigarette butts he picked up off the street illustrates how Einstein's proclivity towards eccentricity could have irreparably damaged his reputation and future. What a loss to mankind would have ensued if this had happened! But at the least, being at the time a well known and often recognized figure, the odds are that members of the public watched Albert Einstein smoke filthy cigarette butts from the street and as a result altered their opinion of this eccentric genius in an uncomplimentary way.

Another mark of Einstein's nonconforming eccentricity was exhibited in the early 20th century when he deserted his wife and two young children for years, subsequently divorced her, and then married his own first cousin. Though divorce and even deserting one's own children is not altogether an uncommon occurrence today, at the time such behavior was not widely accepted.

What do you think most epitomized Albert Einstein's eccentric nature, or, did he possess these seven attributes of eccentricity in a fairly equal measure?

(1) Nonconforming Attitude

(2) Creative

(3) Intense Curiosity

(4) Idealistic

(5) Highly intelligent

(6) Opinionated

(7) Outspoken

Chapter 12

NIKOLA TESLA

"The scientists of today think deeply instead of clearly. One must be sane to think clearly, but one can think deeply and be quite insane."

Nikola Tesla

Nikola Tesla (Born July 10, 1856, Died January 7, 1943) was a Serbian American inventor, electrical engineer, mechanical engineer, physicist, and futurist best known for his contributions to the design of the modern alternating current (AC) electricity supply system. He was also known for the eccentricity of his personality and behavior, but this aspect of Tesla's nature has been relegated to a back seat with little understanding that his eccentricity was the source of many of his greatest inventions, as will shortly be seen.

Tesla gained experience in telephony and electrical engineering before emigrating to the United States in 1884 to work for Thomas Edison in New York City. Because he was not dominated by fear and believed deeply in his own creativity, he soon struck out on his own with financial backers, setting up laboratories and companies to develop a range of electrical devices. Tesla's seeking his fortune on his own terms instead of maintaining the security of his position with Thomas Edison showed a great deal of courage on Tesla's part and was reflective of his very idealistic nature. Nikola Tesla did not create his inventions solely for pecuniary gain but primarily because he wanted to help improve the quality of life of the citizenry of his day.

After Nikola Tesla decided to strike out on his own he had multiple successful inventions. His patented AC induction motor and transformer were licensed by the renowned George Westinghouse, who also hired Tesla for a short time as a consultant. His work in the formative years of electric power development found him involved in a well publicized corporate 'alternating current/direct current' *"War of Currents"* as well as various patent battles.

Nikola Tesla's patented AC (alternating current) inventions stood in direct opposition to the accepted and then utilized method of supplying electricity through direct current (DC). Tesla's invention of the alternating current motor and transformer was an innovative and radical departure from the accepted methods of supplying electricity and was indicative of his nonconformist spirt and immense creativity. Tesla was also a vigorously outspoken proponent of his AC invention and other inventions of his. His life and work provide clear evidence of a nonconformist, outspoken, creative, highly intelligent, extremely curious and idealistic individual.

Tesla's inventions in his chosen field of electricity were enormous successes on numerous occasions. For example, one of his inventions was chosen for the generation of hydro electric energy at the then new power plant under construction at Niagara Falls.

Nicknamed by the press 'The Wizard', concerning his psychological makeup, a very well known reporter, a Mr. Brisbane, studied not only the man himself as well as his inventions but also his psychological makeup, using sound and well accepted journalistic methods. He concluded through these investigative methods that Nikola Tesla was a man who *"lived inside himself"*. Tesla often used flamboyant methods of proving the efficacy of his inventions when other less sensational methods of demonstrating the validity of his inventions were available. Notwithstanding his flair for flamboyance, his inventions were so creative, varied and voluminous that his penchant for publicity for his inventions was understandable because they usually opposed the existing status quo in whatever scientific endeavor he applied himself to. No amount of flamboyance of presentation of his ideas could ever detract from his genius as a profound thinker or his uniquely original and creative accomplishments as an inventor.

Tesla continued to pursue his innovative ideas of wireless lighting and electricity distribution in his high voltage, high frequency power experiments in New York and Colorado Springs, Colorado, and made early (1893) pronouncements on the possibility of wireless communication with his devices. He tried to put these ideas to practical use in an ill fated attempt at intercontinental wireless transmission, known as his unfinished Wardenclyffe Tower project. In his lab he also conducted a range of experiments with electrical discharge tubes, mechanical oscillators/generators, and early X-ray imaging. He also built the first successfully demonstrated remotely controlled wireless boat.

Tesla's eclectic array of innovative inventions and his lifelong devotion to the creation of new forms of utilizing the power of electricity were emblematic trademarks of his life. He invented things that were previously never even contemplated or were considered impossibilities. His work in the field of electricity and his vibrant belief in the boundless future possibilities of new ways to harness the power of electricity served as a key inspiration for the development of electric cars decades after he passed away. The company that created and manufactured the first ever self driving automobiles was named *Tesla Motors* in honor of Nikola Tesla.

Tesla was renowned for his achievements and showmanship, eventually earning him a reputation in popular culture as an archetypal 'mad scientist'. However, the vast and eclectic range of his scientific knowledge is inconsistent with such an assessment. His patents earned him a considerable amount of money, much of which was used to finance his own projects with varying degrees of success. He lived most of his life in a series of New York hotels through his retirement. Tesla died on January 7, 1943. His work fell into relative obscurity after his death, but in 1960 the General Conference on Weights and Measures named the SI unit of magnetic flux density the 'tesla' in his honor. Personal observations that are anecdotal in nature are not scientific evidence but are also not altogether lacking in merit. On a recent trip to Hong Kong in China in 2016, one lengthy taxi ride I took was in a new Tesla electric automobile. It was of course extremely quiet and also opulent inside and outside. While this Tesla car I was in was not self driving, upon returning to the United States I watched, with almost a childlike amazement, internet, television, and documentary pieces that explained the technology behind Tesla self driving cars and visually showed them in operation on the road.

I mention this anecdotal experience because it reminded me of the fact that even the greatest inventions, like the self-driving Tesla cars, trace their roots back to one person who had a new idea. Tesla's remotely controlled wireless boat was by present day standards of little significance, yet today Tesla's concept of wireless remote control is found in military drones and in smaller drones that deliver packages, in the internet, and in so many other places. Consider for a moment how technologically set back we would be today if not for Nikola Tesla. Inventors however are still frequently mocked and belittled, treated as though they were insane and their inventions worthless. I wonder how many incredible inventions there are that people invented in the last five years that have been mocked, disparaged and rejected simply because the inventor was deemed eccentric. Of a surety eccentric inventors are of great value unless we summarily dismiss them as worthless because of their eccentricity.

Turning now to more specific examples of Tesla's eccentric nature, according to friends, associates and contemporaries, Tesla was celibate heterosexually by his own choice because he held the eccentric belief that marriage and love interfered with his work. The nonconformist and courageously outspoken Tesla risked opprobrium when he freely admitted to being sexually attracted to men and worked to develop intimate friendships with men in an era when homosexuality was deemed deviant and an aberration of accepted societal norms.

Another example of Tesla's eccentricity occurred in 1912, when he created and implemented his unconventional plan to, as he put it, *"make dull students bright by saturating them unconsciously with electricity."* Tesla wired the walls of a schoolroom and saturated the classroom with infinitesimal electric waves vibrating at high frequency. Though no dull students were thereby transformed into bright students, he was unafraid to utilize radically unconventional methods to implement his creative and idealistic beliefs. Trying to turn dull students into smart students was at the very least a laudable but extremely eccentric goal that was born of his very idealistic desire to help other people.

The idealistic, highly intelligent and intensely curious mind Tesla possessed, combined with his opinionated and outspoken nature, worked in harmony to make this gaunt, tall man named Nikola Tesla into the scientific genius he was. Throughout his long lifetime his eccentric nature was the driving force that enabled him to question accepted scientific authority and seek better ways for solving problems that beset society. Spurred on by his eccentric nature that cared little what other people thought of him, Tesla courageously persevered and created some of the greatest inventions that made enormous positive contributions to the world he lived in and improved the lives not only of his contemporaries but of generations to follow.

He was known to begin work each day at 3:00 a.m. and continue until 11:00 p.m. This unconventional habit caused him to suffer a serious nervous breakdown at age 25. He then pulled himself together and continued the same regimen well into old age, working for 38 years almost without a break in his rigorous work schedule. He enjoyed spending time with and got along well with pigeons, one in particular. Of this pigeon he wrote that *"I loved the bird: As a man loves a woman, and she loved me. As long as I had her, there was a purpose to my life."* He also had some deep seated and most unconventional revulsions: He couldn't stand overweight women or jewelry of any kind, especially pearls. Nikola Tesla was a true eccentric in every sense of the word.

There has been a resurgence of popular interest in Tesla since the 1990s. If not for Nikola Tesla and his idealistic dedication to improving the conditions under which most people lived, our understanding of electricity would likely be years behind what we now enjoy. Tesla also filed for more than 300 patents for inventions like electromagnets, the radio, and the AC motor. But unlike Einstein, Tesla didn't start out eccentric. His eccentricity followed a more gradual progression as he aged, according to contemporaries. But whether an eccentric's nature bursts forth from childhood or follows a more linearly incremental pathway, their innate disposition towards eccentricity sooner or later becomes an integral part of their persona and life.

It has been said of inventors that when they get it right they are acclaimed as geniuses, but when they get it wrong are dismissed as insane. Nikola Tesla was eccentric but by any reasonable standard of measurement wasn't insane. For example, today when we work on our computers, the Tesla Coil he invented provides the high voltage for the picture tube of computers, and the electricity for present day computers emanates from Tesla's AC generator, which is sent from a transformer invented by Tesla, and arrives at your home or business or wherever you keep your computer by what is known as '3-phase Tesla power'.

In 1943 John G. Trump, a professor at MIT, after reviewing Tesla's voluminous papers delineating his inventions, concluded that both idealism and Tesla's illusions shaped his creative approach unto the very end of Tesla's life. Like any eccentric it is possible to on occasion go too far. For example, Tesla unrealistically persuaded himself that he would be the first man to fly; unfortunately for him Orville and Wilbur Wright beat him to it.

The contributions of Tesla to science can never be denied, as he played a major role and was often the sole source behind inventions that changed the world, such as alternating electrical current, radio, radar, robotics and many more scientific advancements. But it was alleged by "experts" (retrospectively of course; Monday morning quarterbacks didn't begin with the NFL) that he suffered from one or more mental disorders, and as in the cases of Galileo and Vincent van Gogh, most of his peers and the public never viewed his life in the context of the attributes of an eccentric person. Tesla's genius was recognized but unfortunately the public believed that Tesla was an insane genius. The probability that he was instead an eccentric genius who possessed all seven attributes of an eccentric person was never afforded to him:

(1) Nonconforming attitude

(2) Creative

(3) Intense curiosity

(4) Idealistic

(5) Highly intelligent

(6) Opinionated

(7) Outspoken

A few more examples of Tesla's eccentricity include the following:

He did not like to touch anything that even had a small fragment of dirt on it, and it was his practice to walk around a building three times before entering into the domains of the building.

In 1937 while taking his daily walk around Manhattan in New York Tesla was hit by an automobile but refused medical treatment for the injuries he sustained. He continued to decline physically and his eccentricity became even more visible, and by 1940 he insisted on keeping almost everyone at least three feet away from him because of his belief that this was essential to avoid contracting other people's germs.

Nikola Tesla's brilliant intellect is a matter of indisputable historical record. But, was his odd behavior nothing more than the product of a mind suffering from obsessive compulsive disorder or some other psychological aberration, or was he instead an idealistic intellectual genius whose very greatness stemmed from his eccentric mind?

Chapter 13

WINSTON CHURCHILL

"You have enemies? Good. That means you've stood up for something, sometime in your life."

Winston Churchill

Sir Winston Leonard Spencer Churchill, (Born November 30, 1874, Died January 24, 1965) was a British statesman who was the prime minister of Great Britain from 1940 to 1945 and again from 1951 to 1955. Churchill was also an officer in the British Army, a prolific historian, an artist and a writer. He wrote a series of books about the history of England, and after World War II during his five year interregnum from the office of prime minister he wrote a complete account of World War II. He won the Nobel Prize in Literature, and was the first person to be made an honorary citizen of the United States. He was the recipient of so many other honors bestowed upon him that keeping track of them all could be a tedious diversion so I shall spare the reader a complete accounting of them. Besides, for him all his accolades paled next to the part he believed he was fortunate to play during World War II in defeating the Nazi onslaught that sought to enslave the world in a cruel and inhuman tyranny.

Churchill was born into the family of the Dukes of Marlborough, a branch of the Spencer family. His father, Lord Randolph Churchill, was a charismatic politician who served as Chancellor of the Exchequer. It was felt by many that he would one day become prime minister. However, he chose to resign as Chancellor of the Exchequer upon a matter of personal principle, and he never recovered politically. Winston Churchill's mother, Jennie Jerome, was an American socialite. As an aside, it is interesting that a man who is considered a quintessential example of an Englishman and a symbol of Great Britain was actually half British and half American.

When Churchill was a young army officer, he saw action in British India, the Sudan, and the Second Boer War. He gained fame as a war correspondent and wrote newspaper articles and books about his campaigns. He was also captured by the enemy during the Second Boer War and succeeded in making a daring and dangerous escape, which first brought Churchill to the attention of the British public.

At the forefront of politics for fifty years, his humongous, gargantuan and extraordinary intellectual prowess was evident early on in his long and diverse political career and as an author. Churchill, also a competent pilot, could apply his great intellect to almost any project despite how different the issues were than those that he had previously grappled with. For example, he even taught himself to be a master bricklayer and built many beautiful walls and enclosures at his country estate.

He held many political and cabinet positions, so numerous that it is with some reticence they are recounted herein for fear of boring the reader. But his service to the British government was so extensive it deserves a brief summary, because omitting the voluminous history of his government service would diminish an accurate understanding of the sheer magnitude and varied scope of accomplishments of a man who dedicated his life to serving his country.

Before the First World War, he served as President of the Board of Trade, Home Secretary, and First Lord of the Admiralty for the Liberal Party Prime Minister Henry Asquith's government, changing his original party membership in the conservative Tory Party to the Liberal Party. Of this switch in party membership to join Prime Minister Asquith's government, Churchill later often joked about his starting off as a conservative Tory Party member, then becoming a member of the Liberal Party, and then rejoining the conservative Tory Party again. When he was criticized for switching political parties, he responded with quick-witted, insouciant and cleverly inane retorts such as *"It's a woman's prerogative to change her mind"*, and *"I changed parties once, so why not do it again?"* It was very unusual for a politician of Churchill's stature to change parties twice and was indicative of his non-conformist spirit.

Churchill, a very prominent figure in British politics most of his life, was quick to be outspoken not only about issues of import and significance but upon any matter that he believed strongly in, oftentimes outspokenly deflecting criticism in a brilliant and frequently humorous manner. Churchill had an excellent sense of humor and frequently creatively employed it throughout his lifetime, especially during the dark days of World War II.

During the First World War, he served as First Lord of the Admiralty until his planning and execution of what was known as the 'Gallipoli Campaign' ended so disastrously that it caused his abrupt and forced departure from government. Immediately after leaving Henry Asquith's government, he briefly and bravely resumed active army service on the Western Front as commander of one of the Battalions of the Royal Scots Fusiliers, the 6th battalion, and narrowly and by sheer chance (God's providence according to Churchill in a letter to his wife Clementine) avoided being blown to pieces by a German grenade that exploded within less than 200 feet from where he was standing and where he in fact would have been standing had he not been stopped to answer a question.

Interrupting the chronology of Churchill's government service for the first of many excursions into the eccentricity of Winston Churchill, at his country estate named Chartwell, Churchill once spent two complete hours demonstrating with wine glasses and decanters how the Battle of Ireland was fought. Getting worked up like a schoolboy, according to an undergraduate student at Oxford who was present, James Lees-Milne, Churchill also made barking sounds as a dog would to imitate the sound of gunfire and blew cigar smoke across the battle scene reenactment to mimic smoke emanating from guns!

He returned to government under Liberal Prime Minister David Lloyd George as Minister of Munitions, Secretary of State for War, Secretary of State for Air, and then Secretary of State for the Colonies. After two years out of Parliament and once more a member of the Tory Conservative Party, he served as Chancellor of the Exchequer in Prime Minister Stanley Baldwin's Conservative government of 1924–1929. Churchill's returning the pound sterling in 1925 to the gold standard at its pre-war parity was a very controversial and nonconformist decision that was derided at the time by his critics as the action of an unbalanced mind, but his gold modifications succeeded in creating beneficial deflationary pressure on the British economy.

Winston Churchill was out of office and politically 'in the wilderness' during the 1930s because of his opposition to increased home rule for India and because of his staunch resistance to the 1936 abdication of King Edward VIII, who abdicated the British throne to marry an American divorcee. His opposition to home rule for India has been justly cited as an example of a racist streak in Churchill. However, others have postulated that with respect to his stance on India he was not motivated by racism but by his admiration for all things British and his deep loyalty to the government and people of Britain.

Churchill was extraordinarily intelligent as well as opinionated and outspoken throughout his adult life, qualities that were on full display when he took the lead in warning about Nazi Germany and in campaigning for the rearmament of Great Britain. He proved to be perspicaciously prescient in his warnings about the threat of a heavily rearmed Germany, and at the outbreak of the Second World War on September 1, 1939 he was again appointed to the powerful position of First Lord of the Admiralty by Prime Minister Neville Chamberlain.

On May 10, 1940, Prime Minister Neville Chamberlain resigned. Chamberlain made the mistake of traveling to Germany in 1938 and making an agreement with Adolph Hitler known as the Munich Agreement, signed on September 29, 1938. The Munich Agreement allowed Hitler to annex the Sudetenland, the German speaking part of Czechoslovakia and an area that included parts of Germany before their defeat in World War I. This dismemberment of Czechoslovakia was severe because the Sudetenland contained Czechoslovakia's vital border defenses, banks and their heavy industrial areas. In return Hitler agreed to never invade or annex another country. Earlier that same year, in March 1938 Hitler had invaded and annexed Austria to Germany, declaring that Austria no longer existed and was now an integral part of Germany.

Prime Minister Chamberlain returned to London from Germany after signing the Munich Agreement with Adolph Hitler and announced his success in getting Hitler to agree to stop invading and annexing other countries, declaring that he had obtained *"peace in our time."* Much of the British public believed that Chamberlain had sold out the innocent country of Czechoslovakia and made a foolish agreement with a brutal dictator, and that Chamberlain was motivated by fear of a heavily rearmed and aggressive Nazi Germany. Hitler quickly broke the agreement by invading Poland on September 1, 1939.

Historians do acknowledge Chamberlain's good intentions but he is remembered today only as the *'author of appeasement'*. Appeasement of any nation that threatened Great Britain was anathema to Great Britain as the British Empire, with the full support of the British people, had a long history of never bowing to the aggression of any foreign nation.

When Prime Minister Chamberlain resigned on May 10, 1940, by nightfall of the same day Winston Churchill became Prime Minister with tremendous public support. His speeches and his radio broadcasts were brimming with a confidence that helped inspire the British resistance, especially during the difficult days of 1940-41 when the British Commonwealth and Empire stood completely alone in actively opposing and defying Adolf Hitler. He led Britain as Prime Minister until victory over Nazi Germany was secured.

After his Conservative Party lost the 1945 election, at age 70 he became Leader of the Opposition to the Labour Government. At his age and in light of being tossed out of office by the voters within mere months after leading them to victory over Nazi tyranny in World War II, many if not most men or women in his position at this time in their life would have quit politics forever. But Churchill was doggedly determined to remain a voice for the values he believed in, and though few remember today his second tenure as prime minister of Great Britain, from 1951 - 1955, throughout his lifetime he was an example not only of a perseverant spirit but of unrelenting courage.

During his tenure as Leader of the Opposition from 1945 - 1951 Churchill publicly warned of an "Iron Curtain" of Soviet influence in Europe and promoted European unity as a way to counteract the Soviet Union's domination of eastern Europe. His warnings about the ever increasing control of eastern European nations by the Soviet Union received much more attention on the world stage when he returned to the post of prime minister in 1951. However, because Great Britain was no longer a superpower after World War II, Churchill lacked the power to transform his warnings about Soviet encroachment into Europe into any meaningful opposition capable of ending the domination of Eastern Europe by the Soviet Union. Instead his second term as prime minister was preoccupied by non-European foreign affairs, including the Malayan Emergency, the Korean War, the Mau Mau uprising, and a UK backed coup d'état in Iran.

Domestically his government laid great emphasis on house building. Churchill suffered a serious stroke in 1953 and retired as Prime Minister in 1955, although he remained a Member of Parliament until 1964. Upon his death at the age of 90 in 1965, Queen Elizabeth II granted him the honor of a state funeral, which saw one of the largest assemblies of world statesmen in history. Named the Greatest Briton of all time in a 2002 poll, Churchill is widely regarded as being among the most influential people in British history, still consistently ranking well in opinion polls of Prime Ministers of the United Kingdom. Churchill's indomitable courage, a hallmark and binding thread of true eccentrics, was omnipresent through his lifetime. History records countless examples of Winston Churchill's possessing in abundance the seven attributes of eccentric people, listed below for your convenience:

(1) Nonconforming Attitude

(2) Creative

(3) Intense Curiosity

(4) Idealistic

(5) Highly intelligent

(6) Opinionated

(7) Outspoken

For Winston Churchill, courage exemplified his spirit throughout his life. An integral part of Churchill's nature, his courage was on prominent display during his unrelenting defiance of Nazi tyranny during World War II. As the binding thread of the seven attributes of eccentric people, Churchill's courage is worth examining first before delineating Churchill's eccentricities. Before Churchill was prime minister, when he was Chancellor of the Exchequer, a post in Great Britain analogous to the Secretary of the Treasury in the United States, he wrote of an incident concerning two British subjects in China:

At the beginning of 1927, Chinese warlords attacked British subjects in two Chinese ports. The Cabinet decided to send reinforcements to China. Churchill approved, stating: *"Short of being actually conquered,"* he wrote to Prime Minister Stanley Baldwin while on holiday in Eze, France, *"there is no evil worse than submitting to wrong and violence for fear of war. Once you take the position of not being able in any circumstances to defend your rights against the aggression of some particular set of people, there is no end to the demands that will be made or to the humiliations that must be accepted."* This was the essence of Churchill's criticism of appeasement from weakness.

In 1934, in a debate in Parliament on air defense, it was said of Churchill that:

'Churchill did not allow mockery to deflect him.'

In 1940, as Prime Minister of Great Britain after succeeding Neville Chamberlain, the infamous author of appeasement of Hitler, Churchill gave a now famous speech on May 13th in the House of Commons that epitomizes the intrinsic and unrelenting courage and idealistic nature that was at the core of his being:

"You ask, what is our policy? I will say: It is to wage war, by sea, land and air, with all our might and with all the strength that God can give us; to wage war against a monstrous tyranny, never surpassed in the dark, lamentable catalogue of human crime. That is our policy. "You ask, what is our aim? I can answer in one word: victory, victory at all costs, victory in spite of all terror, victory, however long and hard the road may be; for without victory there is no survival. Let that be realized; no survival for the British Empire, no survival for all that the British Empire has stood for, no survival for the urge and impulse of the ages, that mankind will move forward with its goal. "But I take up my task with buoyancy and hope. I feel sure that our cause will not be suffered to fail among men. At this time I feel entitled to claim the aid of all, and I say, 'Come then, let us go forward together with our united strength."

Almost endless examples of Churchill's courage exist, and the purpose of this book is not to record again the complete life of Winston Churchill in biographical form. But one more reference to Churchill's courage is not unwarranted:

Speaking on June 4, 1940 in the House of Commons, Churchill spoke these words, now regarded as one of the finest perorations in history:

"Even though large tracts of Europe and many old and famous States have fallen or may fall into the grip of the Gestapo and all the odious apparatus of Nazi rule, we shall not flag or fail.

"We shall go on to the end. We shall fight in France, we shall fight on the seas and oceans, we shall fight with growing confidence and growing strength in the air, we shall defend our island, whatever the cost may be. "We shall fight on the beaches, we shall fight on the landing grounds, we shall fight on the fields and in the streets, we shall fight in the hills; we shall never surrender. "And even if, which I do not for a moment believe, this island and a large part of it were subjugated and starving, then

our Empire beyond the seas, armed and guarded by the British fleet, would carry on the struggle, until, in God's good time, the New World, with all its power and might, steps forth to the rescue and the liberation of the Old."

Let's examine now some specific examples of Churchill's eccentricities. It was a not uncommon practice for Prime Minister Churchill, completely nude in his bathtub filled with water, to dictate to his secretary. Much has been written about Churchill's drinking habits and his consumption of large amounts of alcoholic beverages was probably his greatest vice. A friend who often used to visit him in the morning at a flat he had in Morpeth Mansions near Victoria, said of Churchill that he always greeted him with a glass of sherry. For lunch there was beer, and at tea time he had whisky instead of tea. Churchill consumed alcohol on a daily basis in not insignificant quantities, especially so for a prime minister of England. He endlessly sucked on the cigar which now bears his name, and during World War II, conducted his private phone calls with United States President Franklin Roosevelt while sitting on his private toilet!

On a trip to Washington, D.C., Churchill, not being accustomed to traffic driving on the right side of the road instead of the left side as in Great Britain, looked the wrong way at an intersection and was struck by an oncoming automobile and hurled to the pavement. Well into his upper 60s at the time, any relatively 'normal' person would regard the accident as serious, take time off and make his personal health and recovery his prime priority. Instead Churchill brushed off the incident and missed none of his planned itinerary for his trip to Washington made at the invitation of President Roosevelt for the purpose of together forging further strategies to defeat the Axis powers.

Also during World War II and again in his late 60s, Churchill suffered a heart attack, an event confirmed by his physicians. Churchill, in true Churchillian fashion, dismissed the heart attack as trivial and after a very brief rest continued his daily schedule essentially unabated.

If we were to remove the name of Winston Churchill from the above incidents and insert any other name of someone who was not a famous public figure, say for example John Smith, many people would probably regard such behavior as insane. Wouldn't it instead be better if people possessed a clear understanding of eccentricity, including the fact that eccentricity is different than insanity? Fortunately for Great Britain Winston Churchill's eccentricities were not only tolerated by his Cabinet and generals in the military, but looked upon with a certain affection.

Winston Churchill is clearly an excellent example of the positive contributions eccentric people can make, but he is also an example of how invaluable it can be in times of critical crises to have at the helm an eccentric person; this may seem to some counterintuitive to what is called 'common sense'. But what is deemed 'common sense' is sometimes not common sense at all but the product of a dull and unimaginative mind that is incapable of perceiving the enormous scope and value of being eccentric.

During the height of the Nazi Luftwaffe aerial bombing of London, Liverpool and other cities and towns, when blocks upon blocks of buildings were reduced to rubble and thousands of British people of all ages died, once the bombing subsided Churchill would personally go to the bomb ravaged neighborhoods. The German aerial bombardment blitz of Great Britain was one of its darkest hours. Churchill responded compassionately, by speaking to crowds of survivors with effusive courage and optimism, lifting their spirits with his ebullient and vibrant personality and manner of speech. Recall that an outward manifestation of eccentric people is their ability to inspire and bring encouragement to the lives of other people.

Thus, perhaps the better part of wisdom would be to think twice or thrice when encountering behavior not considered 'normal' by the mass of society and examine the behavior, thoughts, ideas and values of those we deem eccentric *on their merits* instead of dismissing them by virtue of their eccentric nature as either insane or worthy of no further consideration. One can only speculate how much has already been lost to mankind by eccentric people being disregarded and disparaged. Fortunately Winston Churchill was judged on his merits and not summarily rejected because of his eccentric nature, thereby enabling him to play a vital and consequential part essential to freeing the world from the shackles of Nazi tyranny and preserving democracy for generations to come.

Chapter 14

PABLO PICASSO

"Everything you can imagine is real."

Pablo Picasso

Pablo Picasso (Born October 25, 1881, Died, April 8, 1973), was a Spanish painter, printmaker, ceramicist and sculptor. He was also a poet and playwright; it is notable that writing poetry and being a playwright have little or nothing to do with art painted on a canvas. Therefore, we can glean from these facts alone that Picasso was highly intelligent and extremely creative, reflecting a range of abilities similar to what in an earlier age would have been known as a *Renaissance Man* (a term defined herein previously in chapter six on *Martin Luther*).

Although born and raised in Spain, Picasso spent most of his adult life in France. As one of the greatest and most influential artists of the 20th century, he has been credited for numerous cutting edge advancements in the field of art. For example, he is known as the co-founder of the Cubist movement, the co-inventor of collage, the inventor of unusual modes of sculpture, and for an eclectic variety of styles that he pioneered.

Opinions do vary in assessing his work, but there is a consensus that his two most famous works and those for which he is best known are the proto-Cubist *Les Demoiselles d'Avignon* (1907), and *Guernica* (1937), a portrayal of the bombing of Guernica by the German Luftwaffe on April 26, 1937. The bombing was carried out at the behest of General Francisco Franco of the Spanish Nationalist movement during the Spanish Civil War that began in 1936 and ended in 1939.

Picasso, Henri Matisse and Marcel Duchamp are given significant credit as the three artists who most defined the revolutionary developments in the plastic arts in the opening decades of the 20th century and were also the driving force responsible for very significant developments in painting, sculpture, printmaking and ceramics. Picasso is well known by devotees of art for his part in establishing the Cubist movement.

Picasso was highly intelligent, curious, extraordinarily creative, idealistic, opinionated, outspoken, and displayed a very nonconformist attitude toward life through his unconventional paintings. A famous painting of his had women with rearranged faces and lopsided breasts, one of many of Picasso's paintings that were radically different than what then dominated the art world. Picasso's creative, nonconformist personality can be observed from his early days as an artist, but did not come to full fruition immediately. Additionally, because Realism was still in vogue during a good portion of Picasso's life, many disdained his work because he 'strayed' from a realistic approach to art.

It has been argued by harsh critics of Picasso that his paintings that were done outside of the realm of Realism or Impressionism or post-Impressionism, especially the ones that showed women with disfigured breasts and twisted body shapes, were painted primarily because Picasso was trying to gain more attention, fame and fortune by shocking art critics and the public. No one could have gotten into Picasso's mind back then, but such unique works of art can clearly be seen as emanating from a very creative and nonconformist spirit. Throughout history and irrespective of the field, whether it be art or government or music or religion or any other discipline, when new ground is broken in the quest for something better, banal and provincial minds are quick to condemn anything that disrupts the status quo. The attitude that motivated the disparagement of Picasso for his avant-garde paintings was the same misguided attitude that dismissively denigrated other nonconformist, eccentric people like Vincent van Gogh, Lord Byron, Mahatma Gandhi and John Lennon.

Picasso demonstrated extraordinary artistic talent in his earlier years, when he painted in a naturalistic manner through his childhood and adolescence. This raises the question of whether eccentrics are born eccentric, or, did the events of their lives act as catalysts that triggered their latent and dormant eccentricity? I have no answer to this question beyond speculative opinions. However, irrespective of either the catalysts or causal factors behind their eccentricity, the lives lived by Picasso and by the eleven other historical figures examined in this book all bear record of the presence of the seven attributes of eccentric people:

(1) Nonconforming attitude

(2) Creative

(3) Intense curiosity

(4) Idealistic

(5) Highly intelligent

(6) Opinionated

(7) Outspoken

During the first decade of the 20th century, Picasso's style changed as he experimented with different theories, techniques, and ideas. His work is often categorized into periods. The names of many of his later periods are debated and argued over because what else do art critics have to do with themselves besides engage in endless debates *ad nauseam* about matters so arcane and of so little interest to most people that one wonders if the multitude of beautiful works of art would be better appreciated by the public if art critics didn't exist! Art critics sometimes seem hell bent on focusing primarily on minutia undecipherable by most people who simply enjoy looking at a beautiful or unique painting or sculpture.

However, I would be remiss if I did not include the fact that the most commonly accepted periods in his work are the Blue Period (1901 - 1904), the Rose Period (1904 - 1906) the African influenced period (1907 - 1909), Analytic Cubism (1909 - 1912), and Synthetic Cubism (1912 - 1919), also referred to as the Crystal period.

Try a quick game with your friends by asking these questions after reading aloud the previous paragraph:

(1) How many periods did Picasso's works cover?

(2) What are the names given to these periods of Picasso's work?

(3) What years did each of these periods of Picasso's work cover?

(4) Who the hell cares about the answers to the first three questions?

Did you get many or any of the first three of these four questions right? Would it not be much more worthwhile to seek understanding of Picasso's extraordinarily diverse and creative works by an effort to discover _why_ Picasso was so successful and what might be the underlying force within Picasso responsible for his success?

Exceptionally prolific throughout the course of his long life, Picasso achieved universal renown and immense fortune for his revolutionary artistic accomplishments, and became one of the best known figures in 20th century art. Notwithstanding, some people, including those with PhD's in art, have contended that instead of being an artistic genius Picasso merely scammed everyone for his own personal benefit by purposely creating paintings that would shock the art world. The majority opinion is of course that the various distinctively different works of art he created were a product of his uniquely creative artistic genius.

Many of Picasso's paintings were representative of his intellectual acumen and his fertile and eccentric mind, revealing a man unafraid to push the boundaries of then extant conventional beliefs in the artistic community. Among such paintings that were representative of his nonconformist spirit was a painting of five women portrayed in a very ugly and distorted manner; they looked as if they were about to fall into pieces. It caused quite a controversy with many people (especially art critics) because they thought that it should have looked much more realistic and professionally done. Some art critics went so far as to say that this painting was a complete mockery of art. Picasso had broken all the rules while creating this painting, but his self stated goal was to try and paint the women from more than one angle at a time, hoping that the viewer saw more than what met the eye.

Picasso was different from other artists of his time inasmuch as his art emanated not only from his personal life but sprang forth from his opinions about world affairs. Extremely idealistic and intelligent, he was not afraid to challenge existing beliefs on issues that had nothing to do with art, such as war and peace. One of the political issues that he expressed in paintings focused on the Spanish civil war, a military revolt against the Republican government of Spain that was an outcome of a polarization in Spanish politics that had developed over the previous decades.

In April 1937, Germany, who had transformed itself into a militaristic state on the verge of World War II, sided with the insurgent General Francisco Franco in the struggle for control of Spain during the Spanish Civil War. On April 26, 1937 Germany bombed the town of Guernica in northeast Spain, not far from where Picasso grew up. More than sixteen hundred people were killed and almost nine hundred more were injured.

Highly opinionated and idealistic and outspokenly outraged by the murder of all these innocent people, Picasso decided to paint his most famous painting to date, *Guernica*. Picasso chose to paint *Guernica* in black, blue, and white oil tones; he felt such somber yet strident colors best portrayed the suffering of people and animals, as well as the damage to buildings that the bombing of Guernica created.

Another one of Picasso's many prolific accomplishments was a poster of a dove he painted for the Peace Congress after the Second World War. After surviving three wars, Picasso realized how important it was to work for peace in the world, and because of Picasso the dove is now one of the most important symbols of peace around the world.

Picasso was an eccentric, innovative and perplexing man, a free spirit who was never afraid to dream, imagine, or limit himself by conforming to then accepted artistic norms and standards, which Picasso viewed as barriers to the advancement of art, barriers that he was most willing to break because he viewed them as stifling his creative expression and circumscribing the ability of the art world to see beyond the constrictions of conventional standards. Picasso was not only unafraid of breaking barriers in the art world, he was equally unapologetic for the things in life that he was passionate about, including not only art but war and peace.

And now your analysis is requested: Did Pablo Picasso fulfill the attributes of an eccentric person?

(1) Nonconforming Attitude

(2) Creative

(3) Intense Curiosity

(4) Idealistic

(5) Highly intelligent

(6) Opinionated

(7) Outspoken

Pablo Picasso was one of the greatest figures of the 20th century, a man who had a singular knack for genius in the world of art. He influenced art not only with his unique style, but through the vast amount of sculptures and paintings that he created. Picasso also inspired many other artists in their own respectable art movements because of his passion for setting his own standard for what he wanted regardless of whether or not prevailing public opinion was at odds with his beliefs. Today, even as the name of Einstein is equated with intellectual genius, the name of Picasso is commonly utilized as a synonym for an artistic genius.

One might not be fond of his works or find them confusing, but there is no doubt that without Pablo Picasso, modern art and the world would not be what it is today. His numerous accomplishments impacted not only the historical era that he lived in, but also the future of how the world saw art. *But, would Picasso the artist have ever succeeded in forging his way to the top of the art world without Picasso the eccentric?*

Chapter 15

MAHATMA GANDHI

"Live as if you were to die tomorrow; learn as if you were to live forever."

Mahatma Gandhi

Mohandas Karamchand Gandhi (Born October 2, 1869, Died January 30, 1948) was the preeminent leader and indisputable face of the Indian independence movement in British ruled India. Employing nonviolent civil disobedience, he was an individual who was nonconformist, outspoken, highly intelligent and quite possibly the most idealistic and eccentric public figure India has ever known.

Gandhi's belief in non-violence as the best means of achieving any goal was an essential part of the core of his spiritual beliefs, which were based on religions that included Christianity and Buddhism but were predominately predicated largely on the teachings of the timeless Indian 'bible', the Bhagavad Gita, from which Gandhi drew not only his faith in non-violent means of achieving any goal but also his intense idealism and his eccentricities.

Before exploring the usual salient biographical facts of Gandhi's life, the ability to understand Gandhi as a man is best served by commenting briefly on the outward manifestations of his deeply held spiritual beliefs. Accordingly, Gandhi's biographical synopsis will not proceed along a strictly chronological path. In 1930 Gandhi wrote to the British Viceroy for India that he was going to launch a non-violent resistance to the British statute that made the sale and manufacture of salt illegal, even though salt was essential to the diet in India's hot tropical climate. His non-violent method of protesting British laws about the sale and manufacture of salt were eventually effectuated by a march to the sea to collect sea salt.

Organizing a non-violent march to the sea to illegally collect sea salt epitomizes well Gandhi's firm belief that violence is incapable of ending violence and only provokes further violence. Gandhi believed that if he adhered completely to non-violence in thought, speech and deed, his greater goal of obtaining India's freedom was assured. This was quite an idealistic belief, and it goes to show that idealism is not some foolish concept that never works in the 'real world'. The constraints of the biographical facts of Gandhi's life being limited herein to a synopsis unfortunately makes impossible the inclusion of countless profound and even poetic statements Gandhi made about non-violence throughout his life.

Despite Gandhi's noble and self sacrificing commitment to non-violence and his depriving himself of the comforts and amenities that he could have had as a London trained lawyer, like every person who ever lived Gandhi was not without his faults. Historians have accurately contended that he had a very high sexual appetite which manifested itself more than once. But some critics went so far that they even accused Gandhi of 'forcing', by the power of his stature in India, young adult girls to sleep naked with him alongside his naked body. All the notable eccentrics examined in this book were, as is anyone, imperfect human beings with their share of foibles and human weaknesses and Gandhi was no exception. But if we focused primarily on the failings of any great person or any human being, the enormous contributions Gandhi and others like him made to society would be obscured.

Gandhi began his adult life as a lawyer, having been educated and trained in the law in London, England. His idealism and concern for the welfare of others that characterized his entire life after he abandoned his life in London as a lawyer first manifested itself when he traveled to Africa to help the plight of Indians living in South Africa. He then continued the same quest throughout India. Gandhi was jailed often both in South Africa and in India for his efforts to obtain fair treatment of Indians. This eventually evolved into Gandhi leading a nationwide movement for political freedom and independence from Great Britain.

Atypically, Gandhi considered jail not a hardship but a badge of honor. He was incarcerated frequently for his nonconformist, non-violent protests that provided a voice for the millions of Indians who suffered under India's reprehensible caste system. At the very bottom of the caste system in India was a group of people that were called 'Untouchables', objects of derision and scorn that received harsh treatment by the British and members of higher levels in the caste system such as the Brahmins. Gandhi fought against this system that impoverished millions of Indians, and in so doing helped his people understand that the capacity to suffer bravely for a higher ideal was the only source of strength that would one day make every man and woman in India free and equal. Beginning with his first trip to South Africa to help Indians living there, Gandhi's idealistic nature never wavered.

In eschewing the easy life he could have had as a successful London trained lawyer, Gandhi instead dedicated his life to the mammoth task of freeing his people from British colonial rule and chose to do so by living amongst his people as they lived: poor and suffering under oppressive British rule. The ultimate nonconformist in the annals of India's modern history, Gandhi single handedly defied the great British Empire out of an unfeigned love for his people.

But Gandhi was also quite eccentric. His personality revealed an opinionated, outspoken nonconformist, a man who was highly intelligent, curious and deeply idealistic. Before addressing specific behavioral manifestations that reflected Gandhi's eccentricity, it is important to keep in mind that Gandhi was genuinely *idealistic*. Various examples of his eccentric beliefs and behaviors that are provided herein can only be understood and placed in proper perspective by first realizing that his eccentricities emanated from a heart whose motivation and preeminent purpose was always the same: *Gandhi's desire to help other people.*

Our examples of Gandhi's eccentricities begin with the fact that he kept order for himself by devoting an excruciating attention to detail and to time. He was punctual literally to the minute and expected everyone who came to speak with him, including the most important British minister, to measure up to his own very demanding standards regarding punctuality. Gandhi did not believe in wasting even a grain of rice or a piece of paper. Concerning wasting time, he believed and often stated publicly to the Indian people that our time was not our own but belonged to India as a nation, with people being only trustees for the use of time.

He also had extreme views on food, eating no meat because he was strictly a vegetarian, but no ordinary vegetarian. He concocted his own vegetarian mixtures that were usually not only tasteless but repugnant to eat. He also believed and taught that in order to enjoy life, one must never be selfishly attached to anything, and this included not only money, possessions, prestige or power but also family and friends, believing eccentrically that the natural human love and connection we feel for our family and friends made a person some sort of selfish prisoner to attachment. Yet in spite of all his peccadilloes born of his eccentric mind, his love of the Indian people was real, and he sacrificed his life for them, succeeding eventually in casting off the yoke of the greatest imperial power of his day, the British Empire.

Great Britain required all Indians to export their cotton to England for a pittance to be transformed into cotton in England and sold back to the people of India at prices that were both outrageously high and oppressive. Gandhi's eccentric solution to this was for all Indians to learn the ancient craft of hand spinning cotton into cloth, and even great leaders like independent India's first Prime Minister, Jawaharlal Nehru, spent some part of most days spinning with his own hands cotton into cloth suitable for attire.

Gandhi not only led India to independence, he has inspired movements for civil rights and freedom across the world. The honorific Mahatma, which in Sanskrit means "venerable and high-souled", was applied to him first in 1914 in South Africa and is now used worldwide. He is unofficially called the 'Father of the Nation'.

Born and raised in a Hindu Merchant caste family in coastal Gujarat, in western India, after his return to India from South Africa in 1915, being very idealistic, he organized peasants, farmers, and urban laborers to protest against excessive land taxes and discrimination. After assuming political leadership of the new Indian National Congress in 1921, Gandhi led nationwide campaigns for easing poverty, expanding women's rights, building religious and ethnic comity, ending untouchability, but above all for achieving independence for India.

He lived modestly and whenever possible in a self sufficient residential community. Gandhi's mode of dress was inconsistent with his background as a London trained lawyer; it was however representative of his desire to associate himself with the overwhelming number of the poor populace of India. In addition to eating simple but strange vegetarian food, he also undertook long fasts as a means of both self-purification and social protest, and usually slept only three hours a night. Gandhi also engaged in extended, self-imposed fasts that were not typical practices of the general Indian populace.

Gandhi's vision of an independent India was based on religious pluralism, but was challenged in the early 1940s by a new Muslim nationalism that was demanding a separate Muslim homeland carved out of India. Eventually, in August 1947, Britain acceded to Gandhi's demands and granted independence to India, but the British Indian Empire was partitioned into two dominions, a Hindu majority India and Muslim Pakistan. As many displaced Hindus, Muslims, and Sikhs made their way to their new lands, religious violence broke out, especially in the Punjab and Bengal provinces.

Deciding not to attend the official celebration of independence in Delhi, Gandhi, instead of comporting himself in a manner consistent with self aggrandizement, visited the affected areas where violence was occurring, attempting to provide solace to the people affected by the various outbursts of violence. In the months following, he undertook several fasts unto death to promote religious harmony, an eccentric tactic taken by him to effectuate his deeply held and idealistic belief in rectifying the religious prejudice that plagued the entire sub-continent of India. The last of these fasts, undertaken on January 12, 1948 at age 78, also had the indirect goal of pressuring India to pay out some cash assets owed to Pakistan. Some Hindu Indians thought Gandhi was too accommodating to Muslim Pakistan. Gandhi's death was at the hands of a staunch Hindu nationalist who assassinated Gandhi by shooting him in the chest at point blank range on January 20, 1948.

His birthday, October 2nd, is commemorated in India as *Gandhi Jayanti*, a national holiday, and is remembered worldwide as the International Day of Nonviolence. Advocates of non-violent protest who followed in Gandhi's footsteps, like Dr. Martin Luther King, Jr., were deeply affected by Gandhi's belief that non-violent protest was the only means of defeating injustice and oppression.

Even though he was married at the age of 13 and had four children, Gandhi's eccentricity extended not only to his odd sleeping habits and diet, but as was briefly mentioned earlier, included his views on sexuality. Being charitable to Gandhi we could say that at the very least his pronouncements concerning sexuality were dichotomous, arguably hypocritical, and certainly very eccentric. As a man who was married his entire adult life and who also fathered children, he regarded and taught celibacy as the only way for a man to avoid draining his "vital fluid". Indeed, he spoke about it at length during his sermons, once linking a "nocturnal emission" of his own to the problems in Indian society. Gandhi's public pronouncements advocating that men should be celibate were not just dichotomous conundrums but were in fact hypocritical. According to Jawaharlal Nehru, independent India's first prime minister, Mahatma Gandhi's public statements on sex were *"abnormal and unnatural"* and *"can only lead to frustration, inhibition, neurosis, and all manner of physical and nervous ills… I do not know why he is so obsessed by this problem of sex"*.

Many people, quite understandably, considered Gandhi's beliefs both odd and inconsistent with staid and then accepted methods of addressing the problems facing the Indian nation. However, in Gandhi's lifetime his eccentricity was never appreciated as the integral element of his persona that played the most significant part in fueling his successful quest to free his people.

Gandhi was an outspoken opinionated nonconformist all of his adult life. His curiosity, combined with his high degree of intelligence and creativity, enabled him to discover unconventional methods of protesting British rule of India. His idealistic nature combined with his courageous spirit empowered him to act upon his beliefs and bring to fulfillment his goal of a free and independent Indian nation.

Although some of Gandhi's unconventional ideas were rooted in ancient Hindu philosophy, it has been argued that he was perhaps greatly influenced by the late Victorian age, both in his puritanism and in his unusual theories about health, diet and communal living. Like other epic figures from his not too distant past, such as Leo Tolstoy and Queen Victoria, today he is increasingly perceived in ways that would have surprised his contemporaries. It is unfortunate that like so many great figures in history, only retrospectively did the peculiar ways of Gandhi receive widespread acceptance.

Gandhi has become, in India and around the globe, a simplified version of what he was: a smiling saint who wore a white loincloth while the 20th century eccentric John Lennon wore long hair and distinctive spectacles. Gandhi was a man who ate little, fasted frequently, and succeeded in bringing down the crown jewel of the great British Empire through his then new and unconventional method of practicing non-violent civil disobedience.

Which of the seven attributes of an eccentric person do you think most characterized Gandhi's life?

(1) Nonconforming Attitude

(2) Creative

(3) Intense Curiosity

(4) Idealistic

(5) Highly intelligent

(6) Opinionated

(7) Outspoken

Chapter 16

RAYMOND BURR

*"My greatest satisfaction in acting on television is
to have the opportunity to communicate with the world."*

Raymond Burr

Better known as the iconic television character *Perry Mason,* who he portrayed on television from 1957 until 1966 and again in numerous TV movies from 1985 until his death from cancer in 1993, Raymond William Stacey Burr (Born May 21, 1917, Died September 12, 1993) was a Canadian-American actor who was primarily known for his title roles in the television dramas *Perry Mason* and *Ironside.*

Our examination of the life of Raymond Burr, an eccentric soul who is not as widely known to the world as an Albert Einstein or John Lennon are, begins with a brief but revealing digression concerning Burr's interactions with actor Paul Picerni, who guest starred in several episodes of the first *Perry Mason* TV series. Picerni also contemporaneously co-starred prominently as Federal agent Lee Hobson in the long running American television series *The Untouchables,* portraying the right hand man to Eliot Ness, played by actor Robert Stack. Eliot Ness was a real life famous federal agent who battled against violations of Prohibition and organized crime figures like Al Capone in the 1920s and 1930s. The point here is that Paul Picerni was at the time of his encounter with Raymond Burr already a very well known television actor.

During the filming of one of Paul Picerni's guest appearance on *Perry Mason,* Picerni subsequently recounted in his autobiography his interaction with Raymond Burr during filming of an episode he guest starred in on the first *Perry Mason* television series. In Paul Picerni's autobiography, written a few years before his death in 2011, he recounted how Raymond Burr, secretly at the time gay, flirted openly with him on the TV set off camera but in the presence of other people who were in the same room as Burr and Picerni.

Paul Picerni, who was heterosexual, recounted that this experience for the first time in his life made him feel what women must feel like when hit on or flirted with by a man. Specifically, using the vernacular of his era, he said that Burr's flirting with him made him feel for the first time in his life *"like a broad"*. Raymond Burr was definitely, as his flirting with another man illustrates, unafraid to buck the then status quo.

Today Raymond Burr's openly flirting with Paul Picerni would seem like no big deal in light of the U.S. Supreme Court in 2015 ruling that same sex marriage is legal in all 50 states. But in the late 1950s and early 1960s attitudes towards homosexuality were markedly different, making Burr's flirtatious overtures to another man reflective of a very nonconformist individual.

Further weight is added to Raymond Burr's outspoken nonconformist spirit when one considers the fact that William Hopper, who co-starred as Perry Mason's private investigator Paul Drake in the 1950s-60s TV series, was the son of the then renowned Hollywood gossip columnist Hedda Hopper. Burr was fully aware that the mother of his co-star William Hopper could have exposed Burr's sexual predilections and destroyed his career overnight. Burr's willingness to take that risk in an era when homosexuality was deemed perverted illustrates a courageous and nonconformist individual unafraid to express and act upon his beliefs. Raymond Burr's being gay was kept a carefully guarded secret amongst the cast of *Perry Mason*, but Burr still took huge risks that no one in the cast would publicly reveal his homosexuality.

In that era, to be outed as being a homosexual would have meant the end of Burr's portrayal of *Perry Mason* and likely his entire career as an actor. The filming schedule for the show was brutal, with Burr working 16 to18 hour days 6 days a week, giving the cast and crew of the show ample opportunity to realize that he was gay.

A brief word regarding Raymond Burr's creativity is worth mentioning. Although Burr did not write any of the scripts for the television *Perry Mason* series, *Perry Mason* would likely have been canceled after its first season if not for the incredible creativity Raymond Burr poured into his portrayal of Erle Stanley Gardner's fictional lawyer. *Perry Mason* was already a successful radio program for many years before the first television series hit the airwaves in 1957. Raymond Burr became a presence in the television series, the visible embodiment of a fictional character already well known to the public.

Raymond Burr became *Perry Mason,* and, *Perry Mason* in a sense became Raymond Burr. The two were intertwined because Burr used his own creative mind to infuse every line spoken, every gesture, every step taken, every mannerism, and every action with such creative believability that for an hour the viewing public was gripped by the courtroom dramas to such an extent that Raymond Burr all but vanished from their consciousness and they saw only *Perry Mason.* Further support for Burr's enormously creative portrayal of *Perry Mason* occurred years later when *The New Perry Mason* television series, starring actor Monte Markham as *Perry Mason,* began airing but was abruptly canceled in its first season. Iconic fictional characters usually survive the actor who first portrayed them; for example, the James Bond movie franchise did not end when Sean Connery left the role of James Bond. However, no one has ever revived the character of *Perry Mason* either in film or television since Raymond Burr stamped his indelible mark on the famous fictional TV lawyer. Episodes of the original *Perry Mason* TV series are still broadcast on cable television in much of the United States.

Raymond Burr battled with obesity throughout his lifetime, eventually tipping the scales on his 6'0" frame at well over 300 pounds. When auditioning for the role of *Perry Mason,* he was told to lose weight and return afterward for a second audition. Burr's solution to his portly problem? An eccentric diet of chain smoking cigarettes and consuming only cottage cheese. His unusual solution to his weight problem was though both creative and successful.

That Burr was also idealistic with respect to his own values is attested to by his working for free as a director for the Pasadena Playhouse after becoming famous as *Perry Mason,* and by his contributing substantially to numerous charities. Burr also donated his own time and talents for free to entertain American troops in Vietnam during the Vietnam War. Raymond Burr also exhibited his idealistic nature by becoming involved with real life law enforcement with the Los Angeles Sheriff's Department, using his influence as TV's *Perry Mason* to assist the maintenance of law and order in the real world.

In his second TV series after *Perry Mason* ended its run on television, Burr starred from 1967 to 1975 as Robert T. Ironside, a special consultant to the San Francisco Police department after a 20 year career as a San Francisco police officer and San Francisco police Chief of Detectives was ended when in the line of duty he was paralyzed from the waist down by a bullet and confined to a wheelchair.

Noteworthy to his eccentricity, when on the set during typical very long days filming *Ironside*, regardless of whether he was involved in the shooting of a scene or not, he stayed in character during the entire day's arduous filming of *Ironside* by insisting on remaining inside Universal Studios sets in his wheelchair and refusing to go outside to shoot any outdoor location scenes, which caused coworkers to regard him as odd or peculiar. Correctly identified, this act of Burr's was eccentric.

That Burr was highly intelligent can be observed from the creativity he put into every performance as an actor, his consummate skill as an orator, and his success as a businessman who created a thriving and profitable winery in California with his longtime partner and lover Robert Benevides. Burr married actress Isabella Ward on January 10, 1948, in a marriage of convenience intended to quell rumors that Raymond Burr was a homosexual. They divorced in 1952, and neither ever remarried. In the mid-1950s, Burr met Robert Benevides, a young actor and Korean War veteran, on the set of the *Perry Mason* TV series. According to Benevides, they became a committed couple around 1960. Benevides gave up his own acting career in 1963 and later became a production consultant for over twenty of the *Perry Mason* TV movies. Raymond and Robert were discreet in their relationship, and the *Perry Mason* cast helped conceal Raymond Burr's homosexuality during the entire original 1957-1966 television series and during the *Perry Mason* television movies that ran from 1985 until his death in 1993.

Although *Perry Mason* was a fictional lawyer created by real lawyer and author Erle Stanley Gardner, in all of the *Perry Mason* episodes, genuine California law and in the later television series genuine Colorado law was utilized by Burr and played a vital part in the success of *Perry Mason*. Additionally, Burr's perseverance and dedication to the authenticity of the *Perry Mason* television episodes was evident by the fact that he remained at the top of his game for the entire nine-year run of *Perry Mason*.

When I was in law school it was for three years following the required four years of the college pre-law program, and a three year law school program remains the length of law school programs to this day. It is hardly a stretch of the imagination to conclude that Raymond Burr, in filming episodes of *Perry Mason* over a 36 year period, likely knew more about the law and trial procedures than many newly minted law school graduates and probably some attorneys. This conclusion is attested to by the fact that Burr, an actor and not a real attorney, was a frequent guest speaker at conventions of the American Bar Association (ABA), the national organization of lawyers, from whom he received many ABA awards as well.

Additionally, in her 2013 memoir United States Supreme Court Justice Sonia Sotomayor wrote that the fictional character of *Perry Mason* was a significant impetus in her decision to go to law school and become an attorney. Erle Stanley Gardner, the creator of *Perry Mason*, believed strongly that the various legal issues in every episode must be accurate. He was able to achieve this goal by obtaining final script approval for every episode of the television show. For example, Gardner hired as part of his staff a writer and producer named Ben Brady, who was a practicing attorney for 10 years before becoming a part of *Perry Mason*, and as his story editor, he hired Gene Wang, who had a law school degree.

Raymond Burr's idealistic nature prompted him to sponsor foster children from South Korea, Italy and Vietnam. His idealistic nature was also evident by his being prominently involved in volunteering with multiple charitable endeavors, such as working on behalf of the USO (United Service Organization). Burr was very opinionated and outspoken about his support for American troops who fought in the Vietnam War. He risked his life to perform for the troops multiple times during the Vietnam War in dangerous battlefield areas, breaking the mold of other performers who entertained the troops from a safe location in Vietnam.

Burr's early acting career included roles on Broadway, radio, television and in film, usually as the villain. His portrayal of the suspected murderer in the Alfred Hitchcock thriller, *Rear Window* (1954), is regarded as his best known film role. He won two Emmy Awards, in 1959 and 1961, for the role of Perry Mason. His second hit TV series, *Ironside*, which ran on television from 1967 to 1975, earned him six Emmy nominations.

After Burr's death from cancer in 1993, his personal life again came into question, as details of his known biography appeared to be unverifiable. Of particular note, his public biography stated that during his short marriage he had a son who died a few years into his marriage, which was not true. In 1996, Burr was listed as one of the 50 Greatest TV Stars of All Time by *TV Guide*. A 2014 study found that Burr was rated as a top favorite actor by Netflix users, with the greatest number of dedicated micro-genre followers.

Raymond Burr is included in this study of eccentricity in part to illustrate the fact that a person doesn't have to be a renowned figure on the world stage like Albert Einstein or John Lennon or Winston Churchill in order to be eccentric. Eccentric souls can just as easily be your friends, co-workers or family members and should be respected for their eccentric nature regardless of the fact that they are common people. Disparaging a common person as a loon or a misfit or an insane person because of their eccentric nature makes one wonder what positive contributions such people might have made to the world around them had they been treated with even a modicum of respect and dignity.

Which of the seven attributes held in common by eccentric people do you think most characterized the life of Raymond Burr?

(1) Nonconforming Attitude

(2) Creative

(3) Intense Curiosity

(4) Idealistic

(5) Highly intelligent

(6) Opinionated

(7) Outspoken

Chapter 17

AYN RAND

"The question isn't who is going to let me; it's who is going to stop me."

Ayn Rand

Ayn Rand, (Born January 20, 1905, Died March 6, 1982), was at birth named Alissa Zinovievna Rosenbaum. Born in Russia, she came to the United States to seek her fortune and become an American citizen. When she landed in New York City, on her way to Chicago and eventually the west coast, she changed her name to Ayn Rand because her surname Rosenbaum was a Jewish name and she feared that her prospects for achievement would be diminished if people knew she was Jewish.

Ayn Rand's decision to leave Russia was prompted by the fact that in 1925 anti-Semitic sentiment in the Soviet Union was increasing. Rand believed that America could provide her with a much better environment for achieving her goals in life. She knew that in the America of the 1920s it was difficult for women to get ahead in what was then a man's world, and that it was even more difficult for a Jewish woman to succeed. The fact that 1920s America presented her with major obstacles of a different nature than she would have faced had she stayed in Russia did not stop her from intrepidly seeking her fortune in the United States.

Ayn Rand eventually became an American citizen. She is probably best known today as a successful novelist, especially for her books *The Fountainhead* and *Atlas Shrugged*. Ayn Rand however was also a very outspoken, opinionated commentator on social and political issues. In expressing her nonconformist beliefs through speeches and other writings she has inspired three generations of Americans, was integral in shaping the Libertarian movement, influenced government economic policy since the presidency of Ronald Reagan, and helped shape the political beliefs of many American conservatives, including members of the U.S. Congress.

Ayn Rand was a fierce believer in and proponent of capitalism. Her ideas concerning capitalism have had a singular effect upon influential economists. Some even believe that her writings were responsible for the creation of the American Tea Party movement that began in 2010, almost thirty years after her death.

Before moving to the United States, when she was 19 years old she obtained a college degree in 1924 from Petrograd State University in the Soviet Union. Had she never written a book in her life the achievement of a woman graduating from college at the age of 19 is itself a testament to her high degree of intelligence. Her degree was in history with a minor in political science. Today in the United States, according to 2015 government census bureau statistics, 33% of Americans have a college degree, the largest percentage since the government started keeping records of education levels of the population. Ayn Rand's obtaining a college degree in 1924 was a significant accomplishment but even more so because she was a woman. In the 1920s the percentage of all Americans with a college degree, including both males and females, was less than 3%. Back in the 1920s the U.S. government census bureau did not keep records of college graduates that included differentiating them by sex. Considering the historical milieu in America in the 1920s and then extrapolating from a historical perspective the 3% figure of all college graduates in America in the 1920s, the number of college graduates in the1920s that were women was probably under 1%.

Upon moving to the United States, Rand first obtained work in Hollywood's movie industry, initially as a screenwriter, and then as a playwright. She was neither financially nor artistically very successful as a screenwriter or playwright, and later described her Hollywood days as "grim" and despised the movie capital of the United States as being dominated by "barbarians". That a young girl from Russia could even find work in the Hollywood movie industry as a screenwriter and playwright is illustrative of both her highly intelligent mind and her creativity, especially when one considers the fact that until she arrived in the United States she could not speak English at all and quickly mastered the language of the country she now called home.

Although her dream of becoming a successful and famous writer did not happen immediately after she moved from Russia to the United States in 1925, she eventually became a successful writer and philosopher. Her interests in life were diverse. For example, she had a play produced on Broadway in 1935 - 1936. Because her plays were met with little critical acclaim and were not financially remunerative enough for her to justify further efforts as a playwright, she then switched gears to writing novels that also initially met with little critical or financial success. After two early novels that were largely ignored, as were her plays even though one became a Broadway production, she finally achieved fame and financial success with her 1943 novel, *The Fountainhead.*

Ayn Rand's creativity was deeply rooted in her nonconformist beliefs. In fact, if asked to summarize what most epitomized the character of Ayn Rand the answer would be a simple one: She was a very outspoken and opinionated nonconformist. Ayn Rand also had a seemingly boundless curiosity about life, and was ever ready to criticize and condemn philosophical or political ideas that she believed to be erroneous. Rand's often harsh judgment of political and philosophical ideas that conflicted with her own beliefs was hypocritical because she expected her own political and philosophical ideas to be accepted as true. Like every human being she had her faults, but judging anyone solely on the basis of their foibles is misguided and obfuscates the totality of the person.

The necessity of looking at the totality of a person in order to derive a correct understanding of them is not confined to people but also applies to objects, ideas, places and situations. A vivid demonstration of this truth, that one must gather as much factual information as is possible before passing judgment on any person, place or thing, occurred for me on a trip to Nepal. I had never been to Nepal before and had conjured up in my mind preconceptions and images of Nepal as some sort of Tibetan fantasy land. Although I was intellectually quite aware of the fact that the entirety of my preconceptions of Nepal were rooted not in reality but in the mystique of the Himalayan mountains and Nepal's close proximity to Tibet, I still held onto them as our airplane made its approach to the runway at Nepal's capital city, Katmandu. The airport was completely surrounded by the picturesque snow covered foothills of the mountains. All of my preconceptions of Nepal as some sort of intriguing, enchanting and mysterious Shangri-La now seemed to be validated.

The airport terminal was one of the most beautiful airport terminals I had ever been in. The terminal walls and doors were made of beautifully carved wood stained in a rich brown color. The ceiling was made of wood and the floors were made of opulent marble squares. Now I was even more certain that I had just landed in an exceedingly beautiful and enchanting country. My preconceived mental constructs of the city of Katmandu found me eager to leave the airport terminal building and step inside this beautiful and exotic country. I exited the airport terminal, caught a taxi and proceeded down a winding road into the city. Instead of a Shangri-La I saw a squalid and filthy city so poor that it rivaled the poorest parts of India and Africa I have been to.

From that day forward the importance of not basing my judgment of any person on any single aspect of their character was reinforced in my mind. I had very foolishly allowed misconceptions of Nepal to flourish in my mind based solely upon an easily observable but tiny part of Nepal, the Katmandu airport. If we observe a flaw in Ayn Rand or anyone and because of that reject any further consideration of that person, we can never know the totality of who they really are.

So what shall we make of Ayn Rand? Her critics called her a money grubbing, selfish egomaniac who cared little about the well being of others. Nothing could be further from the truth. She did often challenge authority but she was motivated by a sincere desire to help other people reach their full potential in life. In so doing, Ayn Rand's ultimate goal was to seek innovative solutions to what she believed was lacking in society.

Whether one agrees or disagrees with Ayn Rand's perspective on life, all of her writings and speeches were fueled by her deeply idealistic nature and her genuine desire to help other people. However, her ideas were a radical departure from then prevailing social, political and economic values and she was not devoid of faults. Accordingly her ideas were often met with scorn and derision. Such a negative reaction to Ayn Rand fails to take into account the good motivation and desire to improve the lives of other people that was the very essence of who Ayn Rand was.

Let's return to our chronological biographical synopsis of her life to obtain a better understanding of Ayn Rand and the eccentric nature that was a key stimulus enabling her positive contributions to society. During the early period in her life in the United States, sometime between 1928 and 1929, Ayn Rand first began showing signs of her outspoken, nonconformist nature with statements like "*pride was not a defect of character*". Her willingness to express her nonconformist and opinionated beliefs, for example her rejection of altruism, grew stronger with the passage of time, making her an increasingly controversial figure.

With respect to the novels that she wrote, she is probably remembered most for her two best selling novels, *The Fountainhead* (1943) and *Atlas Shrugged* (1957). In these two novels she emphasized her faith in and the power of human achievement. She also originated in these novels (and throughout her lifetime expanded upon) a philosophical system that later became a movement known as *Objectivism.*

Objectivism's central themes are varied and vast. In her creation of Objectivism as a movement, Ayn Rand's principle contention was that reality exists independently of consciousness. Objectivism as a movement defined by Ayn Rand believed that individuals have direct contact with reality through sensory perception. She expatiated further on the cardinal tenets of objectivism:

1) A person can attain objective knowledge from perception through the process of concept formation and inductive logic.
2) The proper moral purpose of one's life is the pursuit of one's own happiness, also known as rational self interest.
3) The only social system consistent with this morality is one that displays respect for individual rights embodied in laissez-faire capitalism.
4) The role of art in human life is to transform humans' meta-physical ideas through the selective reproduction of reality into a physical form, a work of art that one can easily comprehend and to which one can respond emotionally.

As can be seen from her four tenets of objectivism, Ayn Rand had a great and a very organized and expansive mind that was ever willing to outspokenly disseminate or defend her nonconformist beliefs. Even though the majority of the public disagreed with or ignored her and the intellectuals of her day were cursorily dismissive of her social, philosophical, and political views, I doubt that anyone remembers even the names of her intellectual critics while her impact on the world continues strongly and unabated unto the present day.

A woman of strong beliefs that were reflected in all her varied endeavors, in 1957 she published her best known work, the novel *Atlas Shrugged.* Afterward, she turned to non-fiction to promote the unique philosophy she developed, also publishing her own magazines and releasing several collections of essays until she died in 1982. Rand strongly advocated reason as the only means of acquiring knowledge, and rejected faith and religion, a controversial and definitively nonconformist and outspoken position to take in a then predominately Christian nation. Many consider her to be a quintessential eccentric soul.

In addition to the fact that she did not believe that human pride was a defect of character, as a supporter of rational and ethical egoism she condemned the initiation of force as immoral, and opposed the concepts of socialism, statism and anarchism. Instead she was a strong proponent of *laissez-faire* capitalism, which she believed was not only the best system of government but the very best method for achieving a person's full potential in life because capitalism was predicated on both the recognition and value of respecting individual rights. She was also eclectic in her many interests. For example, in art, she promoted romantic realism, was sharply critical of most philosophers and philosophical traditions known to her, except for Aristotle and some Aristotelians, and in arguably contradictory fashion also supported the ideas of the classical liberals.

Literary critics received Rand's fiction with mixed literary reviews, and academia generally ignored or rejected her philosophy during much of her lifetime. Still, she remained an influential force to be reckoned with since the publication in 1943 of her novel *The Fountainhead,* and academic interest in her has increased in recent decades. The Objectivist movement attempts to spread her ideas, both to the public and in academic settings. She has been a significant influence among political figures, economists, libertarians and conservatives.

Ayn Rand was definitely outspoken, strongly opinionated, had a marked nonconforming attitude, was indisputably creative, idealistic, possessed of a curious nature, and was highly intelligent, all attributes of an eccentric individual. Never one to be shy about her beliefs, this highly creative, very intelligent, nonconformist woman publicly called homosexuality not only *"immoral"* but also *"disgusting"*, even though simultaneously she was an advocate for the repeal of all laws about homosexuality.

She outspokenly rejected many prevailing norms of her time. She often took controversial stances on political and social issues of the day. These included supporting abortion rights, opposing the Vietnam War and the military draft while simultaneously referring to many draft dodgers as *"bums"*. Rand also supported Israel in the 1973 Yom Kipper War against a coalition of Arab nations declaring the Israelis to be *"civilized men fighting savages"*. Ayn Rand also held the controversial belief that the European colonists and later the United States had a justifiable right to take and develop land from Native Americans. Her judgmental language that called men who opposed the Vietnam War and the military draft bums and draft dodgers was both insensitive and callous. Calling Arabs savages and disparaging Native Americans were blatantly racist statements. Like anyone, Ayn Rand was not without faults and flaws.

Rand's influence upon society and even conservative political figures who would by no means be deemed eccentrics has continued to be pervasive. For example, as the Republican Vice-Presidential candidate in 2012 and as Speaker of the House of Representatives since 2016, Paul Ryan has often cited Ayn Rand as an individual who greatly influenced his thinking on social, economic and political issues, and while not agreeing with her on all of her views, also cited her as a strong influence on the conduct of his own personal mores and manner in which he believes he should conduct his life. Paul Ryan is not alone amongst present day conservative political thinkers who reference Ayn Rand as playing a significant part in the formation of their own conservative or libertarian principles, including but not limited to principles such as self reliance of the individual and the collective responsibility of the United States government to practice sound fiscal and monetary policies.

An enhanced understanding of Ayn Rand or any individual can sometimes be gained by noting how her peers that were not dismissively intolerant of her nonconformist ideas viewed her. Murray N. Rothbard, a contemporary of Ayn Rand, wrote a number of articles about her indicative of the unique effect she had on people. In one article he described her thusly:

> "A little woman with straight hair seeping down on one side of her face, her figure can only be described as protoplasmic, amorphous; her age, too, is indeterminate, but presumably she is in her fifties. She wears a shapeless suit with military shoulders in the height of fashion in Moscow back in 1925. Her eyes are beady and intent, and when she talks, she is invariably curled up, ready to strike."

Leslie Hanscom commented on her in Newsweek in 1961 as follows:

> "After three hours of heroically rapt attention to Branden's droning delivery, the fans were rewarded by the personal apparition of Miss Rand herself – a lady with drilling black eyes and Russian accent who often wears a brooch in the shape of a dollar sign as her private icon...."

Another contemporary of Rand's who had personally observed her, Justin Raymondo, said that "with her flowing cape, intense eyes, and long cigarette holder, she was the very picture of eccentricity. She sometimes wore a tri-cornered hat and carried a golden walking stick."

An argument could be plausibly put forth that Ayn Rand did not possess one of the key seven attributes of eccentric people, *idealism*. This argument would likely be based mostly on her beliefs that the proper moral purpose of one's life is the pursuit of one's own happiness and her rejection of altruism. But idealistic people have frequently embraced ideas that seemed at odds with the generally accepted values society shared. In her own unusual way, her ultimate goal was always the happiness and prosperity of everyone.

Other beliefs of Ayn Rand that are seemingly inconsistent with the precepts of idealism include her opinion that pride was not a character defect, her belief that all religions and faith should be rejected, her contention that Europeans had the right to colonize Native Americans, and her belief that Israel had a right to engage in a war with Arabs because Arabs were little more than savages. Her critics maintained that holding such beliefs disqualified her from being imbued with the true spirit of idealism.

Everyone is entitled to their own beliefs and has the right to have their beliefs tolerated *unless a person's beliefs are intended to cause harm to other people*. When new ideas like Ayn Rand's seem to conflict with conventional wisdom that defines society's concepts of right and wrong or good and evil, a correct assessment of such new ideas cannot be obtained without closely examining two key factors:

1) The *motivation* for creating a new idea, and
2) The intended *objective* or goal that results from implementing a new idea.

The word *idealism* traces its history back to the adjective ***ideal***. According to the Oxford English Dictionary, the definition of the word *ideal* means that which is *"most suitable; perfect; desirable"*. Murderers like Adolph Hitler and Joseph Stalin were definitely not *'suitable'*, *'perfect'*, or by any stretch of the imagination *'desirable'* people. Unlike Ayn Rand, Hitler and Stalin were motivated by evil and intended to cause harm; they were murderers without a conscience. However, it can be legitimately argued that Ayn Rand had some beliefs that were the same beliefs held by despots like Hitler. For example, Ayn Rand was prejudiced against Arabs and homosexuals while Hitler was prejudiced against Jews and homosexuals. But Ayn Rand was still the antithesis of Adolph Hitler because she was never motivated by a desire to hurt other people and her objectives were never nefarious.

Furthermore, when we think of an *idealistic* person, history clearly indicates that *idealistic* people are, with the few exceptions that only prove the rule, **good**, not bad, people who believe in helping other people and in making positive and beneficial contributions to the world. Idealistic law school graduates and newly minted physicians who choose to devote their energies to helping others are routinely called *idealistic*, while law school graduates whose primary objective is to get as personally rich as possible aren't usually considered *idealistic*. If getting rich is your primary goal in life this doesn't in and of itself make anyone with this goal a bad person, because wealth can be used for selfish ends or to help other people. Ayn Rand quite simply rejected commonly held beliefs of her era because she genuinely believed that her beliefs were the most beneficial way to improve one's own life and the lives of other people.

Ayn Rand was *idealistic* because she strived to help others, not cause them harm. Rand's principle motive and objective was to help other people realize their full potential in life and was born of a heartfelt concern for improving and bettering the lives of other people.

Sometimes people are best understood by principles they hold dear and that survive the passage of time as notable quotations. To this end - a better understanding of Ayn Rand - here are just a few of her most famous, pithy quotations, that speak volumes about both her character, nonconformist outlook on life, and an idealistic nature that belies accusations that she was little more than a bigoted racist. Here is Ayn Rand in her own words:

> *"A creative man is motivated by the desire to achieve, not by the desire to beat others."*

> *"The smallest minority on earth is the individual. Those who deny individual rights cannot claim to be defenders of minorities."*

> *"The hardest thing to explain is the glaringly evident which everybody had decided not to see."*

> *"Throughout the centuries there were men who took first steps, down new roads, armed with nothing but their own vision."*

A few of the above quotations are perhaps arcane or esoteric. Yet, they provide another method of understanding the essence of Ayn Rand and help weave a picture of just who Ayn Rand really was. So, does Ayn Rand fit the bill of an eccentric individual? If we judge her only by her flaws, foibles and mistakes, the answer would probably be a resounding no, as it would be for anyone who is judged only by their flaws. But if we judge Ayn Rand circumspectly through the prism of the seven attributes of an eccentric person the answer would be a resounding yes:

(1) Nonconforming Attitude

(2) Creative

(3) Intense Curiosity

(4) Idealistic

(5) Highly intelligent

(6) Opinionated

(7) Outspoken

Chapter 18

JOHN LENNON

"Part of me would like to be accepted by all facets of society and not be this loudmouthed lunatic musician. But I cannot be what I am not."

John Lennon

John Lennon (Born John Winston Lennon, October 9, 1940, Died December 8, 1980) was an English singer, guitarist and song-writer who is primarily remembered as a member of the The Beatles, the most commercially successful band in the history of popular music. Lennon founded The Beatles and along with fellow member Paul McCartney formed a celebrated songwriting partnership. John Lennon also played a significant role in the counterculture of the 1960s and 1970s and the peace movement that evolved out of it. He had a perva-sive and widespread influence not only on music but the world, and much has already been written about his vast, innovative and myriad contributions to music, culture and society. The facts of John Lennon's life are herein presented in the same biographical synopsis format uti-lized previously that focused on salient biographical information in order to explore the nexus between the facts of Lennon's life and the seven attributes of eccentric people.

Lennon was idolized by his fans and is still a revered musical and cul-tural figure. This is reflected by the fact that some of the biographies writ-ten about Lennon extolled his virtues while minimizing his flaws. Accord-ingly, John Lennon can herein be much better understood by not adher-ing to a strictly chronological presentation of his life. So, let's begin in an arguably unusual way by examining some of John Lennon's faults, flaws and foibles before getting to his much celebrated musical genius and his advocacy of peace and love.

Lennon was so unfaithful to his wife Cynthia that out of guilt he even-tually confessed to her that he had slept with hundreds of women, includ-ing mutual friends of theirs. Hardly the paradigm for an upstanding fa-ther, throughout John Lennon's lifetime he largely ignored his first born child and son Julian Lennon despite Julian's numerous attempts over the years to establish a relationship with his father. John Lennon was solely responsible for his estrangement from his son Julian, a separation that lasted until the day John Lennon died. Lennon's callous indifference to his son Julian had such an impact on Julian Lennon that the day John Lennon was pronounced dead in a New York City hospital, when John's wife Yoko Ono phoned 17 year old Julian and asked him if he wanted to view his father's lifeless body, Julian declined to do so.

John Lennon also had a cruel streak to his sarcastic and acerbic sense of humor that caused a lot of pain to other people, especially his closest friends, including the other three Beatles. He was also during periods of his life an egomaniac, as well as an addled heroin addict.

Born and raised in Liverpool, England Lennon became involved in the skiffle craze as a teenager; his first band, the Quarrymen, was formed in 1956 and evolved into the Silver Beatles and in 1960 'The Beatles'. Today people remember John Lennon in the context of The Beatles' commercial success as a band, but The Beatles spent seven years together performing mostly cover songs prior to the release of their first record, *Love Me Do*, in 1963. During those lean years before they became successful, when The Beatles became discouraged it was always John Lennon who acted as a ballast, and whose confident spirit brought encouragement to the other three Beatles, which he would often provide by leading them in a semi comical chant: *"Where are we going boys? To the toppermost of the poppermost!"* You may recall that one of the four benefits of being eccentric is the fact that eccentrics possess a confident spirit that brings encouragement to those whose lives they touch.

When the group disbanded in 1970 and ceased creating music together as a four piece band, Lennon embarked on a solo career. As a solo artist John Lennon wrote and recorded many critically acclaimed songs and albums, such as the albums *John Lennon/Plastic Ono Band* and *Imagine*, and numerous iconic songs such as *'Give Peace a Chance'*, *'Instant Karma'*, *'Working Class Hero'*, *'Happy Christmas'* and *"Imagine'* to name but a very few. Other fans of his music undoubtably have their own favorite songs and albums that John Lennon recorded during his post-Beatles musical career; like all music, the musical quality of the songs he wrote are not defined simply on the basis of their commercial success because musical appreciation is very subjective in nature.

Subsequent to his marriage to Yoko Ono in 1969, he changed his name to John Ono Lennon. Having fulfilled his contractual obligations with EMI Records and Capitol Records in 1975, Lennon disengaged himself from the business of writing and recording music for commercial release for a period of almost five years because he wanted to devote his time to raising his newborn second son, Sean Lennon. Lennon returned to making music five years later in 1980 as a solo artist with his double album named *Double Fantasy*. Though the album topped the charts, many believe this was a result of Lennon's death a short while after the release of *Double Fantasy*. Critics and fans alike judged the album inferior to the songs he created and recorded with The Beatles and during his post Beatles career as a solo artist. John Lennon was brutally murdered by being shot to death execution style by a deranged fan on the sidewalk leading to his home in the Dakota Apartments in New York City less than a month after the release of *Double Fantasy* and ironically only a few days after he signed a copy of *Double Fantasy* for his murderer.

Lennon revealed a rebellious nature and a brilliant and at times caustic and biting wit from childhood that remained an integral part of his personality throughout his life. John Lennon was also opinionated and outspoken since childhood. Eventually his nonconformist nature gained a worldwide audience beginning in 1963 with The Beatles first #1 Billboard hit, *Please Please* Me. Throughout John Lennon's tenure with The Beatles, Lennon's idealistic belief in love and harmony was reflected through his music. He became controversial around 1965 for his comments on Jesus and Christianity and again in 1967, this time primarily as a result of his use of LSD and his newly found interest in transcendental meditation.

Lennon was an intensely curious individual. If you think about it, curiosity is always a precursor to questioning the prevailing status quo and evolving into a nonconformist. John Lennon's curiosity led him to a lifelong earnest quest in search of spiritual enlightenment that manifested itself in a very public way when he and the three other Beatles spent a lengthy period of time in India with the Maharishi Mahesh Yogi to further their spiritual understanding of life. Incidentally, despite rampant speculation through the years, the Maharishi Yogi was *not* related to Yogi the Bear who advocates for fire prevention, or to Yogi Berra, the longtime catcher for the New York Yankees.

The previous bit of levity was not intended to cast aspersions upon anyone but to illustrate the excellent and unusual sense of humor John Lennon possessed. He would frequently deploy inane humor not dissimilar to the absurd statement made implicating the fictional cartoon character Yogi Bear and Yogi Berra with Maharishi Yogi. Lennon had a brilliant mind and recognized that his sense of humor could be incisively caustic and hurt other people. He often defused any hurt feelings he caused by his unusual sense of humor through the use of nonsensical humorous statements.

Like anyone John Lennon had many sides to him. Here are just a few quotations of John Lennon's that exemplified his mischievous and quirky sense of humor as well as his unconventional but loving spirit:

"Part of me suspects that I'm a loser, and the other part of me thinks I'm God Almighty."

"I believe time wounds all heels."

"As usual, there is a great woman behind every idiot."

"Everything is dearer when you're in love."

"If everyone demanded peace instead of another television set, then there'd be peace."

"The more real you get the more unreal the world gets."

"Being honest may not get you a lot of friends but it'll always get you the right ones."

"It matters not who you love, where you love, when you love or how you love. It only matters that you love."

"When I went to school, they asked me what I wanted to be when I grew up. I wrote down 'happy'. They told me I didn't understand the assignment, and I told them they didn't understand life."

Close boyhood and lifetime friend Pete Shotton had this to say about his friend John Lennon:

"John was an exceptionally cocky kid who demonstrated precious little respect for his elders and invariably said exactly what he thought. By the age of nine or ten, he had already honed his now legendary 'rapier wit' to the point that he could usually pro-

vide our parents--or anyone else--with a devastating rejoinder whenever they attempted to put him in his place. John was amusing virtually all the time. In my company, his humor was often deadpan in the extreme; he could make me laugh with just a word, a subtle inflection in his voice, or an almost imperceptible gesture.

"John instinctively gravitated toward the center of attention, and his powerful personality always guaranteed him a large and admiring audience. John was our resident comic and philosopher, outlaw and star. In retrospect, one might say that John, even as a child, viewed the world almost as a surrealistic carnival. Life, to him, was a never ending stage play, and he would discover something bizarre in even the most mundane event. Whether an active participant or simply an observer, John would deliver a running commentary on his surroundings, his precociously caustic remarks underscored by an impish glint in his pale brown eyes."

Lennon's deeply rooted belief in love and peace initially manifested itself through his music during his many years with The Beatles. Songs that Lennon wrote the major portions of, for example the Lennon originated song *All You Need Is Love* and his solo career songs entitled *Love* and the iconic *Give Peace A Chance*, as well as countless other Lennon compositions reflect Lennon's idealistic belief in love and peace.

John Lennon took his idealistic belief in peace, love and harmony to the next level through his political and peace activism and his advocation and use of non-violent means of protest, for which incidentally he cited Mahatma Gandhi as influencing his belief in non-violent protest to effectuate social or political change. In 1971 Lennon moved permanently to New York City, living in the Dakota Apartments in Manhattan. John Lennon's opinionated and outspoken criticism of the Vietnam War resulted in a lengthy attempt by the administration of President Richard Nixon to deport him. Some of the protest songs he wrote such as *Give Peace A Chance* were adopted as anthems by the anti-war movement and the larger counterculture sweeping through the United States in the late 1960s and early 1970s.

As of 2012, Lennon's solo album sales in the United States exceeded 14 million, and as writer, co-writer, or performer he is responsible for 25 number one singles on the US Hot 100 chart. In 2002, in a BBC poll of the 100 Greatest Britons, he was voted eighth, and in 2008, *Rolling Stone* ranked him the fifth greatest singer of all time. Lennon was the lead singer on the first five of The Beatles' consecutive #1 songs. He was posthumously inducted into the Songwriters Hall of Fame in 1987, and into the Rock and Roll Hall of Fame twice, as a member of The Beatles in 1988 and as a solo artist in 1994.

John Lennon cannot be fully understood without at least briefly examining his relationship to Paul McCartney. The musical songwriting partnership that John Lennon and Paul McCartney created in The Beatles was considered one of equality, the fusion artistically of two musical geniuses. There is widespread consensus that Lennon and McCartney were different yet equally proficient in every aspect of their career together as The Beatles. Both Lennon and McCartney were excellent singers, virtuoso guitarists, and incredibly prolific songwriters who created beautiful lyrics and melodies for the songs they wrote. Paul McCartney was different than Lennon musically in that McCartney's music tended to emphasize melody more while lyrical content was of cardinal importance to Lennon, even though both John Lennon and Paul McCartney were musical geniuses when it came to crafting both melody and lyrics.

Lennon's nonconformist nature expanded even further during his tenure with The Beatles and by 1968 Lennon's lyrics increasingly reflected his eccentric nature, containing outspoken opinions about social or political issues. Conversely, Paul McCartney's lyrics usually avoided controversial topics, and this musical difference was a factor in Lennon's eventual disenchantment with McCartney that began as spirited but friendly disagreements and evolved into blatant hostility, with Lennon accusing McCartney of writing lyrics that were nothing more than trite, simplistic pablum. The denouement was Lennon's quitting The Beatles in 1970 so that he could through his own music forge ahead with his nonconformist views free of the constraints that Lennon believed the public image of The Beatles imposed upon him. As the solo artist John Lennon he was free to express the full range of his idealistic beliefs.

Humility was also an integral part of John Lennon's nature. For example, in the song he wrote entitled *'I'm A Loser'* Lennon publicly stated that it was himself who was the loser he was singing about. In the #1 song he wrote entitled *'Help!'* Lennon publicly stated that he wrote *'Help!'* because his life was such a mess and *'Help!'* was his plea for somebody to help him. Lennon also publicly acknowledged that Paul McCartney and George Harrison were better guitarists than he was.

The commercial success of The Beatles that was fueled in large part by John Lennon's eccentric nature was not a fluke of fortune, as is evident by the fact that even today The Beatles are still regarded as the Number 1 pop music band of all time. The Beatles created and triggered a musical, cultural and historical phenomena, the likes of which had never been seen before nor since. From 1963 through 1966 the adulation The Beatles received by the public that often bordered on hysteria was so great that the press dubbed it *'Beatlemania'*. Although The Beatles notable achievements are too numerous to list here, beginning in 1963 with their song *Please Please Me* until the group disbanded in 1970, they had 20 #1 hits on the Billboard charts, and The Beatles still hold the record for the most #1 songs on the Billboard pop/rock music charts. Their albums all peaked at #1 as well. The vision and passion of eccentric people that resided in John Lennon in spades fueled The Beatles meteoric rise to the top of the popular music world.

For the first five years of their career beginning in 1963 every 45rpm record The Beatles released went to #1 until *Penny Lane* peaked at #2 in 1967, and every 45rpm single that The Beatles released subsequent to *Penny Lane* also went straight to the top of the Billboard charts. In 1995 the three Beatles still living used a cassette tape of John Lennon singing and playing the piano to his unfinished composition *Free As A Bird.* Paul McCartney and George Harrison wrote choruses for the song and sang and played electric guitar, bass guitar and keyboards together with Ringo Starr on drums. Their efforts, based upon a John Lennon song released to the public 15 years after Lennon's death, resulted in *Free As A Bird* by The Beatles going to the top of the Billboard charts. When *Free As A Bird* went to #1 in 1995 The Beatles had #1 Billboard records covering a 32-year period, from 1963 through 1995.

The Beatles could have never existed without Paul McCartney, George Harrison and Ringo Starr, and this biographical synopsis of the life of John Lennon is not in any way intended to diminish the contributions of the other three Beatles. But just as The Beatles could have never existed without Paul McCartney, George Harrison and Ringo Starr, neither could they have ever existed without their eccentric leader John Lennon. Together as The Beatles, John Lennon, Paul McCartney, George Harrison and Ringo Starr riveted the music world and the sheer magnitude of the worldwide impact The Beatles had upon music and society was so great that a closer look at The Beatles is warranted in order to better understand John Lennon.

Beatlemania, mentioned earlier, was driven in significant part by John Lennon and saw fans screaming and crying uncontrollably during their concerts. Though such a fan response to a musical group's live perfor-mances was not the first time in modern musical history that an exuber-ant response by fans occurred, the level of fan excitement and reaction far exceeded what had been previously seen in performances by artists like Frank Sinatra and even Elvis Presley. Many believe that this was a result of three factors: the original songwriting, virtuoso musicianship, and first rate singing of The Beatles, a combination of musical abilities never before seen in popular music.

It has been suggested by historians and sociologists that timing was a key impetus behind *Beatlemania*. According to this theory, the appear-ance of The Beatles, then in their early twenties, on television for the first time in The United States in February, 1964 gave renewed optimism and a sense of future promise that seemed to be lost to the country after the assassination of the youthful, charismatic and energetic U.S. president John F. Kennedy only a few short months prior to the February, 1964 appearance by The Beatles on The Ed Sullivan Show, an appearance that was watched by over 60 million Americans and that broke all previ-ous records for the size of a television viewing audience.

Kennedy was succeeded by the much older, colorless and non-charismatic Lyndon Johnson only a few months prior to The Beatles first exposure to a massive U.S. television audience, and The Beatles exem-plified the stark contrast between Kennedy and Johnson and reminded people of the same youthful vigor and optimism President Kennedy is still remembered for. Notwithstanding the serendipity for The Beatles of their introduction to American audiences coinciding with the recent loss of President Kennedy, it was the secret sauce of eccentricity that flour-ished in John Lennon that stoked the fire of *Beatlemania*.

Irrespective of the various reasons postulated for *Beatlemania*, the fact remains that John Lennon was the leader of The Beatles, although Paul McCartney was his equal in every respect. Lennon was a powerful force behind The Beatles, having largely written and sung lead vocals on the first five #1 chart topping records of The Beatles. John Lennon had a successful solo career after The Beatles, but he was first and foremost an inextricable part and driving engine of The Beatles, and through them his intellectual genius and his creativity were on full display for all the world to see.

Examples of John Lennon's eccentric behavior throughout his lifetime are voluminous, but a few examples will illustrate this with cogent clarity. During the height of Beatlemania all four members of The Beatles attended a function in their honor that was held at the British Embassy in Washington D.C. A dignitary at that embassy reception who was standing behind Ringo Starr pulled out a scissors and cut off a locket of Starr's hair without Starr's permission. Ringo Starr was obviously surprised and very upset as a result. John Lennon witnessed this very disrespectful act but declined to follow the decorum of functions at the British Embassy by politely overlooking it. Instead, the attributes of an eccentric person combined with the courage he possessed compelled John Lennon to walk directly up to the British dignitary who snipped off part of Ringo Starr's hair and verbally chastise him for his disrespect and rudeness. Lennon was met with a reply from this British dignitary that his cutting off a locket of Ringo Starr's hair was essentially no big deal. Lennon responded by loudly swearing at him and berating him and then signaled his three bandmates to abruptly leave the reception forthwith, with Lennon continuing to loudly curse the British dignitary with choice four letter expletives as The Beatles departed the embassy together.

Another example of John Lennon's eccentricity occurred early in The Beatles' career but also at the height of their worldwide fame. Lennon made a few off-hand but explosively opinionated and unconventional comments about Jesus and the future of Christianity. He told a reporter for the *London Evening Standard*, Maureen Cleave, in a fairly lengthy interview that *"Christianity will go. It will vanish and shrink ... We're more popular than Jesus now — I don't know which will go first, rock and roll or Christianity."*

Five months after Lennon's comment about Jesus and Christianity to reporter Maureen Cleave of *The Evening Standard*, when the remark was reprinted in the United States, Beatle worship turned to Beatle hatred, with most of it fueled by religious conservatives. Churches held bonfires of their records. The Ku Klux Klan, weirdly assuming the moral high ground, nailed a Beatles' album to a wooden cross and threatened to disrupt an upcoming Beatles concert.

The protest then spread even further to other countries including Mexico, South Africa and Spain. Some radio stations banned their records. The controversy was so serious, erupting as it did on the eve of a Beatles' tour in the United States, that the band's manager Brian Epstein considered canceling it. Lennon apologized in a televised interview in which his genuine sadness was very apparent; he almost began crying.

He tried to explain that he wasn't trying to knock Christianity or God but was only making a factual observation in response to a question posed to him by a reporter.

Many people familiar with the music of The Beatles and John Lennon did not know that he was actually a very spiritual man who believed in a higher power and that that life continued after death. On one occasion he described death as analogous to getting into a taxi on one side, then exiting that taxi on the other side and immediately opening the door and entering into another taxi right alongside the first taxi. His deeply spiritual nature was not only frequently reflected in the lyrics he wrote but also during an extended stay in India seeking spiritual enlightenment with the Indian maharishi who introduced The Beatles to transcendental meditation. During The Beatles' sojourn in India, they were accompanied by many other people, including the songwriter/singer/guitarist Donovan, Mike Love of The Beach Boys, and the well known actress Mia Farrow and her sister.

Few remember John Lennon as the epitome of human kindness and compassion but this was also an integral part of his nature. A telling example of Lennon's kind and compassionate spirit manifested itself during The Beatles' stay in India. Mia Farrow's sister was quite shy and insecure to the point that Lennon noticed that she often stayed alone in her cabin for extended periods of time. Lennon said that his sadness at observing the lack of social skills of Mia Farrow's sister inspired him to write the beautiful and moving song *Dear Prudence,* which became part of The Beatles double album released in 1968 titled simply *The Beatles* but commonly and usually known as *The White Album.* The poignant lyrics of *Dear Prudence* began with an exhortation to her to come out and play followed by noting that the sun was out, the place in India where they were staying was beautiful, and so was she, Mia Farrow's shy sister.

Returning to Lennon's comments about Jesus Christ and God to Maureen Cleave, John Lennon was widely perceived as a rock star who led a typical rock star's life, which included being somewhat of a hedonist and not particularly interested in God, spirituality, or the concept of life after death. To a degree this assessment of Lennon was definitely not without a valid basis in fact, because much like any rock star who becomes extremely famous worldwide and a multimillionaire, he succumbed to the pitfalls of fame and fortune and often indulged his every whim. For example, he used illegal drugs extensively, including marijuana, LSD, amphetamines and heroin during his tenure with The Beatles; in fact for a few years Lennon was a heroin addict. He also drank to excess. On one occasion he and his friend singer Harry Nilsson were thrown out of The Troubadour nightclub in Los Angeles because they were so inebriated they began heckling the performance onstage by the Smothers Brothers. When he met the woman who was for him the very essence of a beautiful woman, Bridgette Bardot, he was so drunk she ended the private meeting with Lennon minutes after arriving at Lennon's hotel room when Lennon made a lewd pass at her. But John Lennon's life and music belied a nearsighted opinion of him that ignores the totality of his character. Public perceptions of famous people are frequently inconsistent with the reality of the lives of the movie or rock stars that people idolize from a distance.

To this day Lennon's bandmate in The Beatles, George Harrison, is remembered as a devoutly spiritual man. George Harrison's music definitely reflected a keen spiritual nature, exemplified in his 1973 Billboard #1 song *Give Me Love*, his #1 record *My Sweet Lord*, and many other songs that he wrote. At the same time however, George Harrison regularly used drugs ranging from marijuana to LSD, was unfaithful to his wife Patti, and even carried on a sexual affair with Ringo Starr's wife Maureen.

John Lennon's life was also filled with a quest for spiritual understanding of concepts of God, including Jesus Christ. In 1969, a year before The Beatles broke up in 1970, one evening, albeit after a few joints, Lennon informed a friend, *"I think I'm Jesus Christ."* His mate replied, *"You what?"*

On another occasion, this time in a restaurant, a gentleman came up to John and said: *"Really nice to meet you, how are you?"* *"Actually,"* said John, *"I'm Jesus Christ."* *"Oh, really?"* said the man. *"Well, I liked your last record."*

Not long before The Beatles split up in 1970, Lennon called for an emergency board meeting of Apple Records, the recording company The Beatles established in 1968 for the release of their records and those of a few other musical artists, including James Taylor and the group *Badfinger*. The other three band members attended, and also present were longtime friend of The Beatles and then Apple's managing director, Neil Aspinall, and Derek Taylor, their press officer.

"Right," said John, *"I've something very important to tell you all. I am...Jesus Christ. I have come back again. This is my thing."* No one could think of what to reply to that. Someone suggested they adjourn for

lunch instead. Then Paul McCartney, consistently the stabilizing force to Lennon's eccentricity, told John that he suggested just keeping this quiet for now, keeping it within the cloistered inner circle of The Beatles. McCartney succeeded in defusing Lennon's outrageous assertion with a stroke of sagacious wisdom, and a crisis that could have been destructive or fatal then to the future of The Beatles was avoided.

McCartney and Lennon were band mates and best friends since their teenage years. A special bond between them existed, in addition to the bond of their mutual love of music, that was forever deepened between them when Paul McCartney's mother Mary died of breast cancer when McCartney was 14 and when Lennon's mother Julia was killed by being run over by a car driven by a drunken, off duty Liverpool policeman when John Lennon was 16.

Paul McCartney had his share of disagreements with Lennon, dissed him in a few post Beatles songs and Lennon responded in kind by including on one of his first solo albums a song he wrote directly to Paul McCartney entitled *How Do You Sleep At Night*. The Beatles were forced by fame to live on top of each other and were often sealed off from the world, literally alone together for many years. Such a circumstance would produce a certain level of rancor among the best of friends. Paul McCartney recognized that John Lennon was at his core an idealistic and loving soul, and expressed his understanding of John Lennon's true nature both publicly and privately, unabashedly speaking often of his friendship and love for his songwriting partner and best mate, both during Lennon's lifetime and after Lennon's death. After John Lennon died, McCartney wrote a moving tribute to Lennon of his love for John entitled *Here Today*. Paul McCartney still performs *Here Today* in concerts, and his deep love for John Lennon often results in McCartney becoming visibly emotional on the stage as he sings and plays his acoustic guitar during *Here Today*.

When John Lennon was shot to death in New York City and died at the young age of 40, since his death in 1980 through today, the extraordinary life of John Lennon and the love and affection millions of people around the world had then and still have for him is remembered frequently in gatherings on the day he was born, October 9th. Perhaps the most prominent theme of these various recollections of the life of John Lennon and his music and spirit is this: a keen awareness and appreciation of the profound positive effects John Lennon had amongst the multitudes of his fans.

John Lennon was, to say the least, unique. He was a far cry from perfect, being a notorious womanizer who not only deeply hurt his wife Cynthia Lennon and their son Julian but was often thoughtless and even cruel to other people, even his fellow Beatles and closest friends. Yet, with all his imperfections, his personality, his talent and his countenance melded together to make him one in a million. But we have to ask this question: What actually made this one human being stand out so brilliantly amongst the crowd? Was it largely his music or mostly his sometimes acerbic yet delightful wit and the outrageous comments made to friends, strangers and the public at large? Or, was it the totality of Lennon's eccentric nature that propelled him to heights not only of musical greatness but as a prominent cultural leader who advocated for peace and inspired millions of younger people around the world. Many have aspired to greatness, yet unlike Lennon, few ever achieve their goal. It is difficult to overestimate John Lennon's eccentricity as a major force behind his success.

The circumspect answer to this question is that his music, his spirit, his soul, and his unique accomplishments all played their part, but Lennon's eccentric personality played the most integral part in his achievements that set him apart from the crowd. A few accomplishments born of his eccentricity included his pioneering a new form of music, a new style of long hair and atypical apparel for men, his part in creating the new counterculture movement, and his proactive social and musical expression of his deeply held beliefs about the value of peace and love. While John Lennon often had an ego in the stratosphere, notwithstanding his eccentric spirit was authentic. He seemed to have lived his life on the edge from the very start, and over the years this carved him into the honest, intuitive, and gritty yet very sensitive artist that much of the world admired and loved.

Eccentric almost from early childhood, John Lennon seemed to sense he had a mission to accomplish, an almost superhuman goal to achieve. And as fate would have it, Lennon did indeed experience the kind of success and fame that comes to few. However, in his youth he was as unknowing as the rest of the world just how his ambition and drive would play itself out. Of his early awareness of his unique nature, John said:

"It was scary as a child, because there was nobody to relate to. Neither my auntie nor my friends nor anybody could ever see what I did. It was very, very scary and the only contact I had was reading about an Oscar Wilde or a Dylan Thomas or a van Gogh--all those books that my auntie had that talked about their

suffering because of their visions. Because of what they saw, they were tortured by society for trying to express what they were. I saw loneliness.

"Surrealism had a great effect on me, because then I realized that my imagery and my mind wasn't insanity; that if it was insane, I belong in an exclusive club that sees the world in those terms. Surrealism to me is reality. Psychic vision to me is reality. Even as a child, when I looked at myself in the mirror when I was 12, 13, I literally used to trance out into alpha. I didn't know what it was called then. I found out years later there's a name for those conditions. But I would find myself seeing hallucinatory images of my face changing and becoming cosmic and complete. This thing gave me a chip on the shoulder; but, on the other hand, I wanted to be loved and accepted. Part of me would like to be accepted by all facets of society and not be this loudmouthed lunatic musician. But I cannot be what I am not."

Lennon, the quintessential eccentric, also epitomized, as have some other eccentrics, both the seven major attributes of eccentrics and the four secondary attributes:

(1) Nonconforming attitude

(2) Creative

(3) Intense curiosity

(4) Idealistic

(5) Highly intelligent

(6) Opinionated

(7) Outspoken

---

*   Sometimes not interested in the opinions or company of other people

•   Mischievous sense of humor

*   Knew in early childhood that he or she was different from others

•   Happy obsession with a hobby or hobbies

John Lennon's possession of the seven attributes of eccentric people is evident even in a truncated biographical synopsis. The facts of his life reveal a man who at the center of his being was a *nonconformist*. Lennon had a musical *creativity* of profound proportions. Those like John Lennon who question the status quo and seek to find new and then unknown alternatives are indubitably possessed of an *intense curiosity* that of necessity is present because it is part and parcel of the intellectual quest for something better than the extant status quo. Lennon's *idealistic* nature expressed itself not only through his songs but through his years of advocacy for changes in society through the means of non-violent protest.

That Lennon was *highly intelligent* is evident from the deep insights he had into numerous complex issues that he resolved and expressed through his songwriting; his musical genius alone reflects his *highly intelligent* nature. John Lennon also possessed a hallmark of *highly intelligent* people, the ability to change his methods of solving problems, e.g., his recognition that heroin was not the way to finding peace in his own soul. Lennon's *opinionated* and *outspoken* nature were an essential part of him from childhood and these two attributes of an eccentric person were ubiquitously evident throughout his lifetime.

As for the secondary attributes of eccentric people, Lennon had a mischievous sense of humor from childhood onward and knew from his early childhood that he was different from other people. Lennon was very sociable and gregarious but at the same time was often not interested in the company of others or their opinions. His happy obsession from childhood with music and playing the guitar and singing began as a hobby but eventually blossomed into his life's work.

In regard to John's keenly gifted nature, there were some early clues, which were evident from a young age and were initially known only to his close friends and family. When The Beatles exploded upon the pop music scene in Great Britain in 1963 and in the United States in early 1964, John Lennon now had an international platform to spread his beliefs, a metaphorical megaphone that he exercised.

John's Aunt Mimi, who raised him instead of his mother Julia, sadly seemed to be the one person who could least appreciate the early signs of John's visionary artistic talent. John never doubted her obvious love for him, but she didn't seem to understand him; but that did come from a few others who were in contact with the young John. At his junior school, when handing Mimi a bundle of John's drawings, John's teacher told her: *"The perspective is amazing for a boy of eleven."* Yet, this didn't stop

Mimi from tossing out John's precociously creative artwork. His Aunt Mimi also told him that he would never make a living playing the guitar. Of this period of his life, John said:

> "People like me are aware of their so called genius at ten, eight, nine. I always wondered: 'Why has nobody discovered me?' In school, didn't they see that I'm cleverer than anybody in this school? That the teachers are stupid, too? That all they had was information that I didn't need. I used to say to my auntie, 'You throw my fuckin' poetry out and you'll regret it when I'm famous,' and she threw the bastard stuff out. I never forgave her for not treating me like a fuckin' genius or whatever I was, when I was a child. It was obvious to me. Why didn't they put me in art school? Why didn't they train me? Why would they keep forcing me to be a fuckin' cowboy like the rest of them? I was different, I was always different. Why didn't anybody notice me? Later on, the fuckin' fans tried to beat me into being a fuckin' Beatle or an Engelbert Humperdinck, and the critics tried to beat me into being Paul McCartney."

These are arguably troubling words and indicative of Lennon's by no means small ego and not altogether infrequent outbursts of anger or frustration, depending on one's point of view. Notwithstanding, there is no question that John Lennon was an extraordinarily creative musical genius, a lifelong nonconformist who revolutionized the music world and became a cultural icon who significantly impacted and shaped the world around him. He was an eccentric and often misunderstood genius, a perseverant soul who defied the odds and rose to the uppermost echelons of music, culture and society.

Chapter 19

WHAT CAN THE MOVIE & TELEVISION INDUSTRIES TEACH US ABOUT THE VALUE OF BEING ECCENTRIC?

"I tried being reasonable, but I didn't like it."

Clint Eastwood

Most people like movies, so much so that the movie making business is a multi-billion dollar industry. People who invest capital in the production of a movie do so at the risk of losing their investment and damaging their careers and the artistic careers of the actors who appear in their movies, which also translates into further financial and personal loss for those involved in the production of a movie. So what on earth you might ask can the movie and television industries teach us about eccentricity? More to the point, do movies and television series reflect an admiration for eccentric people or disparage them?

One of the most successful movie franchises in the world, now over 50 years old, is based on the fictional British spy James Bond. The character of James Bond was actually rooted in reality, as the author of all the Bond novels, Ian Fleming, was during World War II the first British spy commissioned and utilized in the mold of the fictional character of James Bond. Fleming's foray into the job of being the first foreign spy for Great Britain eventually evolved into the present day MI-6, the British spy agency. In all the James Bond novels and movies, Bond works for MI-6 as a foreign spy.

The first Bond movie was *Dr. No*, released in 1962. Since 1962 the James Bond movies have grossed over $7 billion dollars and the film series is the longest continually running movie series in history. Part of the enduring success of the James Bond movies into the 21st century is due to the producers astutely recognizing that the Bond movies give the audience the opportunity to escape into a world where they can imagine themselves as the daring, dashing, heroic character of James Bond, and for the duration of the movie live vicariously through James Bond and escape the problems, doldrums or boredom of their own lives. It is of course true that the James Bond character exists in a fictional world. It is also true that people very frequently look to fictional characters they admire, either in movies or books, to establish a better template for overcoming the difficulties of their own lives.

The fictional character of James Bond has resonated positively with millions and millions of people worldwide. The appeal of James Bond went far deeper than the fact that every actor who portrayed James Bond from Sean Connery onward was a handsome and charismatic man. Hollywood has an abundance of handsome male actors who can easily act the part of a dashing and daring character. So there must be something deeper that extends specifically to the persona of the fictional spy James Bond that audiences gravitated to. Ask yourself the following question: Would James Bond still be James Bond if he did not possess a *nonconformist* spirit? Not only does the Bond character fail to conform to the universal value that one shouldn't kill people, Bond was often at odds with his superiors at MI-6, preferring on numerous occasions to do things his own way. James Bond is endlessly *creative* in devising, often on the spot, unique solutions to seemingly impossible dilemmas that threatened his life. His *intense curiosity* gave him the ability to inquire into situations that seemed simple on their face but were weaved with intrigue and deception. Bond would never have survived much less vanquished his numerous foes absent a *highly intelligent* nature, and his *outspoken* and *opinionated* nature were on constant display. That the British spy James Bond is *idealistic* goes without saying: If you're British you can't get much more idealistic than willingly risking your life for Queen and country.

On several occasions after watching the latest James Bond movie in a movie theater with friends, after exiting the movie theater, we walked to a nearby Starbucks for a cup of coffee and engaged in a discussion about the fictional character James Bond. I asked my friends - without ever once mentioning the word 'eccentric' - three questions. The first question was whether or not they believed James Bond is a nonconformist, highly intelligent, opinionated, outspoken, curious, creative, idealistic character who is the epitome of a courageous man. I asked them whether Bond possessed each personality attribute as a separate question for each attribute with the courage of James Bond being the last question asked. On each such occasion every single person that I queried answered my question in the affirmative - James Bond possessed all seven of the personality attributes that I had just asked them about. I then asked them all my second question: Do any of you personally know anyone in your own life who possessed these seven qualities? About a third of them said they did. Then I asked the 33% that did know someone in their own lives who possessed these seven personality traits my third and final question: What do you think of these people?

The respective answers I received were on every occasion and in varying degrees of intensity the same: they didn't like the person they knew personally who possessed all seven of the personality attributes that they had just agreed that James Bond possessed. We then had an interesting discussion over a few more cups of coffee about the inconsistency of admiring the seven personality attributes with respect to James Bond while having a negative opinion of the people they knew personally who possessed all of the same seven personality attributes that they agreed James Bond is endowed with.

So what can the movie and television industries teach us about the value of being eccentric? The answer to this question is that the movie and television industries rarely make movies or television shows about boring people afraid to take risks or unwilling to rock the boat of acceptable societal norms, but are most willing to produce films about eccentric characters like James Bond because *that which is unique has throughout history been greatly valued* - and James Bond is indeed very unique. Hollywood also understands that movies and television series are well received and profitable when they tap into and fill a void in our own lives.

For example, I speculate that not a few lovers of James Bond movies wish that their own lives were as exciting and daring as Bond's, and though they may not realize it, are full of respect and admiration for a fictional character who in essence is about as eccentric a man as they come! Yet the same people who love James Bond encounter eccentric people in their own lives, and to put it euphemistically, admiration of them is not a word that would describe how they think or feel about them or act towards them. Why?

What does Hollywood know that the general public seems oblivious too?

Perhaps the simplest answer lies in the fact that eccentric people are fascinating - not insane but simply fascinating to people, especially to those who have by choice or default or through no fault of their own found themselves in a rather uneventful or boring existence.

Hollywood is also a profit motivated business, and accordingly the movie and television industries are mainly focused on what will make them a profit while avoiding productions that will result in financial loss. Hollywood long ago realized that they can maximize their profits by focusing on that which is unique - and eccentric people are unique.

One of the many examples illustrating the penchant of the movie and television industries for creating a movie or television series that stars an eccentric person was the American television series 'House', which demonstrated its appeal by being a top rated TV show that ran for eight years on the Fox network. The series starred actor Hugh Laurie.

Hugh Laurie is a British actor who previously had a long running career playing mainly comic roles and sometimes dramatic roles on British television. Laurie perfected a flawless American accent that served him well as he portrayed the fictional American physician, Dr. Gregory House, a cantankerous but lovable genius who possessed all seven attributes of an eccentric person - he was a nonconformist, outspoken, opinionated, curious, creative, highly intelligent and idealistic physician. Dr. House also had two of the secondary traits of eccentrics; a mischievous sense of humor, and, he was frequently dismissive of the opinions of others.

The television series 'House' is just one of many creations of the television and movie industries that are illustrative of the fact that Hollywood almost invariably doesn't give the starring role to boring people. Another excellent example of Hollywood's predilection for placing an eccentric character in the starring role is Clint Eastwood's portrayal of the iconic cop known as 'Dirty Harry'. Eastwood starred as Harry Callahan, an eccentric San Francisco Police Department Inspector. The film series named after the first motion picture 'Dirty Harry' saw Clint Eastwood reprise the 'Dirty Harry' character four times, in 'Magnum Force', 'The Enforcer', 'Sudden Impact', and 'The Dead Pool'. Eastwood parlayed his success as Dirty Harry into numerous subsequent movies in which he also played an eccentric character, including 'Pale Rider' in 1985, which was the highest grossing western of the 1980s, and 2008's Gran Torino. Eccentric characters are valued so highly by the movie making industry and greatly appreciated by fans that rarely does a movie character that is not eccentric ever become a movie franchises such as James Bond.

The long running success in television and movies of the eccentric character created by Sir Arthur Conan Doyle, Sherlock Holmes, is the epitome of an eccentric genius. Beginning with British actor Basil Rathbone first portraying Sherlock Holmes in movies in the 1930s and

1940s, *Sherlock Holmes* movies and television series' have endured. British actor Jeremy Brett portrayed Holmes for many years on television in the 1980s and 1990s, and the series, which aired in both the UK and the USA, only ceased because Jeremy Brett died. Currently British actor Benedict Cumberbatch portrays *Sherlock Holmes* in the latest British television series incarnation of *Sherlock Holmes*. Cumberbatch plays *Sherlock Holmes* in present day 21st century England. The series is entitled *Sherlock* and is a phenomenal success and an internationally acclaimed show. In movies, Robert Downey Jr. has portrayed *Sherlock Holmes* in a successful franchise since 2009's *Sherlock Holmes* and 2011's *Sherlock Holmes: A Game Of Shadows.*

Many movies based upon the lives of real eccentric historical figures such as Mahatma Gandhi have been financially successful and critically acclaimed. Successful movies have also been made wherein the hero of the film is deemed a common yet eccentric individual. There have been so many movies and television series made over the years that citing every movie or TV series featuring an eccentric character would require a very lengthy separate book. Perhaps the most effective proof of the fact that the movie and television industry gives its starring roles to eccentric people and unusual characters *can best be provided by you, the reader,* simply by recollecting some of your favorite movies and asking yourself whether the star or the protagonist of the film was an eccentric character.

If you reexamine some of your own favorite film or television characters and apply the seven essential attributes of an eccentric person to them, I speculate that though you likely were enjoying the movie and popcorn or the comfort of watching television in your own home and were not contemplating the lead character's connection to the unusual subject of eccentricity, the individual(s) you admired and were rooting for to succeed fall within the parameters and paradigm of an eccentric person:

(1) Nonconforming attitude
(2) Creative
(3) Intense curiosity
(4) Idealistic
(5) Highly intelligent
(6) Opinionated
(7) Outspoken

Chapter 20

WHY ECCENTRICITY IN PEOPLE SHOULD BE VALUED

"Do not fear to be eccentric in opinion, for every opinion now accepted was once eccentric."

Bertrand Russell

In the very first paragraph of this book I stated that this is an unconventional book. It seems fitting therefore that this last chapter summarize in an unconventional manner *The Value Of Being Eccentric* by first posing a question and obtaining the answer to this question from some of the brightest and best minds society has ever produced:

Question: *Should eccentric people be valued?*

"In this age, the mere example of non-conformity, the mere refusal to bend the knee to custom, is itself a service. Precisely because the tyranny of opinion is such as to make eccentricity a reproach, it is desirable, in order to break through that tyranny, that people should be eccentric. Eccentricity has always abounded when and where strength of character has abounded; and the amount of eccentricity in a society has generally been proportional to the amount of genius, mental vigor, and moral courage which it contained."

John Stuart Mill

"A person willing to fly in the face of reason, authority, and common sense must be a person of considerable self-assurance. Since he occurs only rarely, he must seem eccentric to the rest of us. A person eccentric in one respect is often eccentric in others. Consequently, the person who is most likely to get new ideas is a person of good background in the field of interest and one who is unconventional in his habits."

Issac Asimov

"I find only freedom in the realms of eccentricity."

David Bowie

"People are quite frequently eccentric."

Jane Smiley

"Eccentrics.....At best the world fails to take them seriously, and at worst it ridicules them."

William B. Irvine

"Eccentricity is not, as dull people would have us believe, a form of madness."

Dame Edith Sitwell

"The world thinks eccentricity in great things is genius, but in small things only crazy."

Edward Buller-Lytton, 1st Baron Lytton

"What am I in most people's eyes? A nonentity or an eccentric and disagreeable man. I should want my work to show what is in the heart of such an eccentric, of such a nobody."

Vincent van Gogh

"Here's to the crazy ones, the misfits, the rebels, the troublemakers, the round pegs in the square holes, the ones who see things differently - they're not fond of rules. You can quote them, disagree with them, glorify or vilify them, but the only thing you can't do is ignore them because they change things, they push the human race forward, and while some may see them as the crazy ones, we see genius, because the ones who are crazy enough to think that they can change the world, are the ones who do."

Steve Jobs

"The worst thing I can be is the same as everybody else. I hate that."

Arnold Schwarzenegger

"Be virtuous and you will be eccentric."

Mark Twain

"Eccentricity comes from the mind and a playfulness about life and language, manifesting itself in real individualistic character."

Coulter Watt

"Never underestimate the stimulation of eccentricity."

Neil Simon

"Eccentricity is what's sexy in people."

Rachel Weisz

"When the purge of individualism is unrestrained, eccentricity, initiative and individuality are the casualties."

Andy Hargreaves

"The surest defense against evil is extreme individualism, originality of thinking, whimsicality, even, if you will, eccentricity."

Joseph Brodsky

"Be daring, be different, be impractical; be anything that will assert integrity of purpose and imaginative vision against the play-it-safers, the creatures of the commonplace, the slaves of the ordinary."

Sir Cecil Beaton

"Never forget that only dead fish swim with the stream."

Malcolm Muggeridge

"Do not fear to be eccentric in opinion, for every opinion now accepted was once eccentric.

Bertrand Russell

"A free society cherishes nonconformity. It knows from the nonconformist, from the eccentric, have come many of the great ideas."

Henry Steele Commager

Eccentric people share in common all - not just some - of the seven attributes of eccentric individuals   :

(1) Nonconforming attitude

(2) Creative

(3) Intense curiosity

(4) Idealistic

(5) Highly intelligent

(6) Opinionated

(7) Outspoken

Eccentric people are *Society's Secret Sauce*, the idealistic, innovative and nonconformist people who boldly shine a light into the darkness of the unknown path that lies ahead. They not only glimpse the future but have played and will continue to play a significant part in forging a better tomorrow for the people that their lives touch. Every person alive today has one thing in common with everyone else around the world: No one knows what tomorrow will bring because the future is unknown. Eccentric people play a significant part in bringing that unknown future world into a better place.

At the beginning of this book four benefits that eccentric people bring to society were listed. They are listed again now:

(1) Eccentricity enables the pursuit of new ideas and modes of thinking.

(2) Eccentrics possess a singular ability to sort out confusion and crystallize the most important issues at hand.

(3) With their unconventional ideas born of courage, eccentrics engender courage in others.

(4) Eccentrics possess a confident spirit that brings encouragement to those whose lives they touch.

These four positive contributions of eccentric people are evident throughout the lives of all twelve people examined in this book. Eccentric people are ubiquitous in the world. Sometimes they are famous and sometimes they are not. But whether eccentric people make their contributions to society on a large scale or their positive impact reaches only to the lives of their friends and family, history records time and again that they have often been the engines of positive and beneficial changes across the broad spectrum of society, that 'secret sauce' of *eccentricity* that has brought and will continue to bring courage, inspiration, the pursuit of innovative ideas, solace, joy, courage and happiness into the lives of countless millions, perhaps even billions of people.

BIBLIOGRAPHY

CHAPTER 1

Ozersky, J. (2012). *Colonel Sanders and the American dream.* Austin, TX: University of Texas Press.

Metz, C. (2011). *This Community of Companions: A History of Bush Brothers & Company.*
Knoxville, TN: Bush Brothers & Company.

Stares, J. (2005, November 6). Einstein, Eccentric Genius, Smoked Butts Picked Up Off Street. London, England: *The Daily Telegraph: History Extra.* Retrieved from *https://www.telegraph.co.uk › News › World News › Europe › Belgium.*

Hilliam, R. (2005). *Galileo Galilei: Father of modern science.* New York, NY: The Rosen Publishing Group

Lipton, J. (2006). *Inside The Actors Studio: Dave Chapelle.* Season 12, Episode 9. February 12, Bravo Cable TV, New York, NY.

Drutman, L. & Drinkard, D. (2012). *The changing complexity of Congressional speech.* Sunlight Foundation. Retrieved from https://sunlightfoundation.com/2012/05/21/congressional-speech.

CHAPTER 2

Raeder, L. (2002). *John Stuart Mill and the religion of humanity.* Columbia, MO: University of Missouri Press.

Glendenning, V. (1981). *Edith Sitwell, A unicorn among lions.* London, England: Weidenfield & Nicholson.

Bartlett, D.L. & Steele, J.B. (1979). *Empire: The life, legend and madness of Howard Hughes.* New York, NY: W.W. Norton & Company.

Census.gov (2000) Census.gov. Retrieved from https://www.census.gov/population/www/cen2000/

CHAPTER 3

Knipping, A. (2012). *Eccentricity.* Self published through amazon.com. Seattle, WA: CreateSpace Independent Publishing Platform.

Weeks, D. & James, J. (1995). *Eccentrics: A study of sanity and strangeness.* New York, NY: Kodansha International.

Glendinning, V. (1981.) *Edith Sitwell: A unicorn among lions.* London: England: Weidenfield & Nicholson.

CHAPTER 4

No additional sources utilized other than dictionary definitions, which are referenced in the body of the text of this chapter.

CHAPTER 5

AllMusic (2013). *Paul McCartney, Charts and Awards.* Retrieved from www.allmusic.com.

Miles, B. (1997). *Paul McCartney: Many years from now.* New York, NY: Henry Holt & Company.

CHAPTER 6

Bainton, R. (2013). *Here I stand: A life of Martin Luther.* Nashville, TN: Abingdon Press. Originally published (1955). New York, NY: Mentor Printing

Works by or about Martin Luther at the *Internet Archive,* https://www.archive.org

Marty, M. (2004). *Martin Luther.* New York, NY: Viking Penguin.

Hendrix, S. (2015). *Martin Luther: Visionary reformer.* New Haven, CT: Yale University Press.

Oberman, H. (2006). *Luther: Man between God and the Devil.* New Haven, CT: Yale University Press.

CHAPTER 7

de Leeuw, R., Editor, van Gogh, V. (1998). *The letters of Vincent van Gogh.* New York, NY: Penguin Classics.

Proverbs 18:14, 1603 King James translation of the Bible.

Naifeh, S. & Jackson, G.W. (2012). *Vincent Van Gogh: The life.* New York, NY: Random House.

Stone, I & Stone, J. Editors, van Gogh, V (1995). *Dear Theo: The autobiography of Vincent van Gogh.* New York, NY: Plume Publishers & Penguin Books.

Doctor Who: Vincent and the Doctor (2010). Season 5, Episode 10. London, England: BBC Television.

CHAPTER 8

Isaacson, W. (2003). *Benjamin Franklin: An American life.* New York, NY: Simon & Schuster.

Lemay, J. & Zall, P., Editors (1986). *Benjamin Franklin's autobiography.* New York, NY: Norton Critical Editions.

Srodes, J. (2002). *Franklin, The essential founding father.* Washington, D.C.: Regnery History.

Lemay, J. (2008). *The life of Benjamin Franklin.* Philadelphia, PA: University of Pennsylvania Press.

CHAPTER 9

Marchand, L. (1957). *Byron: A life.* New York, NY: Alfred A. Knopf.

O'Brien, E. (2009). *Byron in love: A short daring life.* New York, NY: W.W. Norton & Company.

Eisler, B. (1999). *Byron: Child of passion, fool of fame.* New York, NY: Alfred A. Knopf.

Wilkes, J. (2014, November 12). What Pet Did Lord Byron Keep At Cambridge University? London, London, England: *History Revealed.* Retrieved from https://historyrevealed.com.

CHAPTER 10

No additional source material utilized.

CHAPTER 11

Issacson, W. (2008). *Einstein, His life and universe.* New York, NY: Simon & Schuster Paperbacks.

Highfield, R. & Carter, P (1993.) *The private lives of Albert Einstein.* London, England: Faber and Faber.

Rajan, A. (2016, December 21). What Does The Future Hold For The Daily Telegraph?. London, England: BBC News

Brian, D. (1996). *Einstein: A life.* New York, NY: John Wiley.

Stares, J. (2005, November 6). Einstein, Eccentric Genius, Smoked Butts Picked Up Off Street. London, England: Retrieved from: *The Daily Telegraph: History Extra. www.telegraph.co.uk › News › World News › Europe › Belgium.*

CHAPTER 12

Cheney, M. (2011). *Tesla: Man out of time.* New York, NY: Simon & Schuster.

Carlson, W.B. (2013). *Tesla: Inventor of the electrical age.* Princeton, NJ: Princeton University Press.

Burgan, M. (2009). *Nikola Tesla: Inventor, electrical engineer.* Mankato, MN: Capstone Press.

CHAPTER 13

Gilbert, M. (1991). *Churchill, A life.* New York, NY: Holt Paperbacks, Henry Holt & Company.

Jenkins, R. (2001). *Churchill: A biography.* London, England: MacMillan.

Meacham, J. (2004). *Franklin and Winston: An intimate portrait of an epic friendship.* New York, NY: Random House Trade Paperbacks.

CHAPTER 14

Fitzgerald, M.C., (1996). *Making modernism: Picasso and the creation of the market for twentieth-century art.* Berkeley, CA: University of California Press.

Rubin, W. (1981). *Pablo Picasso: A retrospective.* New York, NY: Little Brown & Company.

Berger, J. (1989). *The success and failure of Picasso.* New York, NY: Pantheon Books.

CHAPTER 15

Easwaran, E. (2012). *Gandhi the man: How one man changed himself to change the world.* New Delhi, India: Nigiri Press.

Fischer, L., Editor (2002). *The essential Gandhi: An anthology of his writings on his life, work, and Ideas.* New York, NY: Vintage Books.

Brown, J.M., (1991). *Gandhi: Prisoner of hope.* New Haven, CT: Yale University Press.

Majmudar, U. (2005). *Gandhi's pilgrimage of faith: From darkness into light.* Albany, NY: SUNY Press.

CHAPTER 16

Starr, M.S. (2008). *Hiding in plain sight: The secret life of Raymond Burr.* New York, NY: Applause Theater & Cinema Books.

Hill, O.L. (1994). *Raymond Burr: A film, radio and television biography.* Jefferson, NC: McFarland & Company, Inc.

Picerni, P. & Weaver, T. (2007). *Steps to stardom: My story.* Albany, GA: BearManor Media.

Dougan M. (1986, June 9). Raymond Burr: Much More Than Just Perry Mason. London, England: Retrieved from *The Telegraph, https://www.telegraph.co.uk.*

Erickson, H. (2009). *Encyclopedia of television law shows.* Jefferson, NC: McFarland & Company.

Sotomayer, S.M. (2013). *My beloved world.* New York, NY: Alfred A. Knopf.

CHAPTER 17

Heller, A.C. (2009). *Ayn Rand and the world she made.* New York, NY: Anchor Books.

Branden, B. (1986) *The passion of Ayn Rand.* Garden City, NY: Doubleday & Company.

Burns, J. (2009). *Goddess of the market: Ayn Rand and the American right.* New York, NY: Oxford University Press.

Ryan, C.L. & Bauman, K. (2016). *Educational attainment in the United States.* Washington, D.C.: United States Census Bureau. Retrieved from https://www.census.gov/population/www/education

CHAPTER 18

Coleman, R. (1992). *Lennon: The definitive biography.* New York, NY: McGraw-Hill Book Company.

Emerick, G. & Massey, H. (2006). *Here, there and everywhere: My life recording the music of The Beatles.* London, England: Penguin Books.

Lennon, C. (2005). *John.* New York, NY: Crown Publishing Group.

Miles, B. (1997). *Paul McCartney: Many years from now.* New York, NY: Henry Holt & Company.

Norman, P. (2008). *John Lennon: The life.* New York, NY: Ecco Press.

Rolling Stone, (2008, April 12). *100 Greatest Artists of all Time.* Rolling Stone. New York, NY: Wenner Media LLC. Retrieved from https://www.rollingstone.com.

Spitz, B. (2005). *The Beatles: The biography.* New York, NY: Little, Brown & Company.

Lawrence, K. (2005). *John Lennon: In his own words.* London, England: Andrews McMeel Publishing.

Goldman, A.H. (2001). *The lives of John Lennon.* Chicago, IL: Chicago Review Press.

Martin, G. (1983). *Making music.* London, England: Pan Books.

Cleave, M. (October 5, 2005). The John Lennon I Knew. London, England: *The Daily Telegraph.* Retrieved from https://*www.telegraph.*

CHAPTER 19

Chancellor, H. (2005). *James Bond: The man and his world.* London, England: John Murray.

Pearson, J. (1967). *The life of Ian Fleming: Creator of James Bond.* London, England: Pan Books.

CHAPTER 20

No additional source material utilized.

PHOTO/ILLUSTRATION CREDITS

Winston Churchill
Rare Book Division, The New York Public Library. (1946). The Waldorf-Astoria
Retrieved from http://digitalcollections.nypl.org/items/b6d31c6c-6fb3-cb35-e040-
e00a18061428

Dr. Martin Luther
The Miriam and Ira D. Wallach Division of Art, Prints and Photographs: Print
Collection, The New York Public Library. (1838). Dr. Martin Luther. Retrieved
from
http://digitalcollections.nypl.org/items/510d47da-f9ae-a3d9-e040-e00a18064a99

Benjamin Franklin
The New York Public Library. (1783). Benjamin Franklin. Retrieved from
http://digitalcollections.nypl.org/items/78be0425-f96b-476f-e040-e00a1806784e

Lord Byron
Henry W. and Albert A. Berg Collection of English and American Literature, The
New York Public Library. (1837). Lord Byron. At the age of 19. (From an original
Picture in the possession of Sir John Cam Hobhouse, Bar-t.)
Retrieved from http://digitalcollections.nypl.org/items/510d47db-c142-a3d9-
e040-e00a18064a99

Vincent Van Gogh
Detroit Institute of Arts
Date 1887 ; MediumOil on artist board, mounted to wood panel; Dimensions
Framed: 20 1/2 x17 x2 3/4 in. (52.1 x43.2 x7 cm.) Unframed: 13 3/4 x 10 1/2 in.
(34.9 x 26.7 cm) New York, auction Kélékian (American Art Association) Jan.
30, 1922, lot 100 (bought by the Reinhardt Galleries for the DIA)

Albert Einstein
Photograph by Orren Jack Turner, Princeton, N.J.
United States Library of Congress's Prints and Photographs division under the
digital ID cph.3b46036. Copyrighted 1947, copyright not renewed. Einstein's
estate may still claim copyright on this image, but any such claim would be considered illegitimate by the Library of Congress. No known restrictions.

Nikola Tesla
The photograph image of Nikola Tesla (1856-1943) at age 34.
Date circa 1890
This work is in the public domain in its country of origin and other countries and
areas where the copyright term is the author's life plus 100 years or less. It is in
the public domain in the United States because it was published (or registered
with the U.S. Copyright Office) before January 1, 1923.
Retrieved from: https://commons.wikimedia.org/wiki/File:Tesla3.jpg

Pablo Picasso
The photograph image of Pablo Picasso 1962
This image is in the public domain because the copyright of this photograph, registered in Argentina, has expired. (Both at least 25 years have passed after the photograph was created, and it was first published at least 20 years ago, Law 11.723, Article 34 as amended, and Berne Convention Article 7 (4)).
http://www.magicasruinas.com.ar/revistero/internacional/pintura-pablo-picasso.htm

Ayn Rand
Source (1905-1982) from her Soviet passport
Date 29 October 1925
This work is not an object of copyright according to article 1259 of Book IV of the Civil Code of the Russian Federation No. 230-FZ of December 18, 2006.
Source
http://www.morethings.com/philosophy/ayn_rand/ayn_rand_photo_gallery01.htm

Mahatma Gandhi
Source: http://www.answers.com/topic/mahatma-gandhi-large-image
Date: early 1940's
This work is in the public domain in India because its term of copyright has expired. The Indian Copyright Act applies in India, to works first published in India. According to The Indian Copyright Act, 1957 (Chapter V Section 25), Anonymous works, photographs, cinematographic works, sound recordings, government works, and works of corporate authorship or of international organizations enter the public domain 60 years after the date on which they were first published, counted from the beginning of the following calendar year (ie. as of 2017, works published prior to 1 January 1957 are considered public domain). Posthumous works (other than those above) enter the public domain after 60 years from publication date. Any other kind of work enters the public domain 60 years after the author's death. Text of laws, judicial opinions, and other government reports are free from copyright. Photographs created before 1958 are in the public domain 50 years after creation, as per the Copyright Act 1911.

Raymond Burr
Cropped screenshot of Raymond Burr from the film *Please Murder Me*. (Date 1956)
This work is in the public domain because it was published in the United States between 1923 and 1963 and although there may or may not have been a copyright notice, the copyright was not renewed. Unless its author has been dead for the required period, it is copyrighted in the countries or areas that do not apply the rule of the shorter term for US works, such as Canada (50 pma), Mainland China (50 pma, not Hong Kong or Macao), Germany (70 pma), Mexico (100 pma), Switzerland (70 pma), and other countries with individual treaties.

John Lennon
Bob Gruen, August 29, 1974 New York City
Fotosketch pencil drawing manipulation of inverted original photo, not subject to copyright restrictions.
Source: http://www.manipulating artists.com/lennon-NYC.

Made in the USA
Lexington, KY
14 April 2017